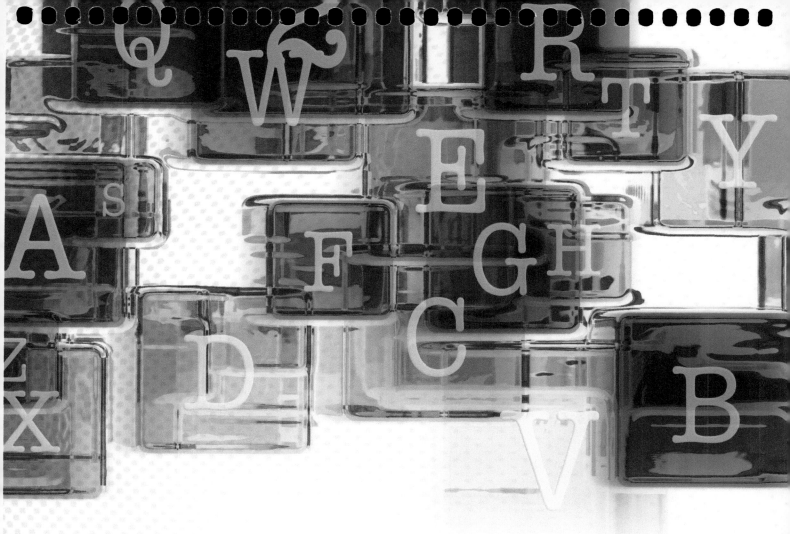

Paradigm

# Keyboarding

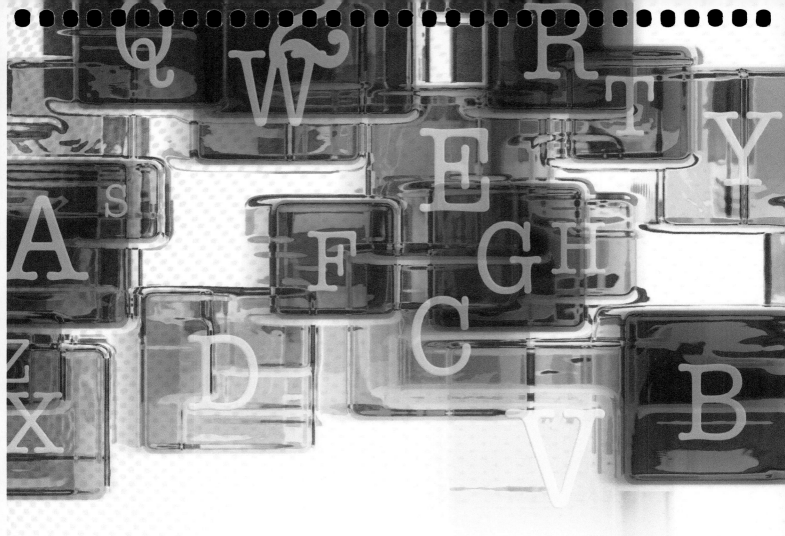

Paradigm

# Keyboarding

## Sessions 1–30

Seventh Edition

**William Mitchell**   ▪   **Audrey Roggenkamp**   ▪   **Patricia King**   ▪   **Ronald Kapper**

PARADIGM
EDUCATION SOLUTIONS

St. Paul

| | |
|---:|---|
| **Division President** | Linda Hein |
| **Vice President, Content Management** | Christine Hurney |
| **Developmental Editor** | Eric Braem |
| **Editorial Support** | Jennifer Gehlhar, Melora Pappas, Katie Werdick |
| **Director of Production** | Timothy W. Larson |
| **Production Editor** | Blaire Wickstrom |
| **Cover Designer and Production Specialist** | Jack Ross |
| **Vice President, Digital Solutions** | Chuck Bratton |
| **Digital Projects Manager** | Tom Modl |
| **Digital Solutions Manager** | Gerry Yumul |
| **Vice President Sales and Marketing** | Scott Burns |
| **Director of Marketing** | Lara Weber McLellan |

Special thanks to the following individuals: Janet Blum, Fanshawe College; Rebecca Born, NorQuest College; and Janet Bradley, Conestoga College.

Care has been taken to verify the accuracy of information presented in this book. However, the authors, editors, and publisher cannot accept responsibility for Web, email, newsgroup, or chat room subject matter or content, or for consequences from application of the information in this book, and make no warranty, expressed or implied, with respect to its content.

**Trademarks:** Microsoft is a trademark or registered trademark of Microsoft Corporation in the United States and/or other countries. Some of the product names and company names included in this book have been used for identification purposes only and may be trademarks or registered trade names of their respective manufacturers and sellers. The authors, editors, and publisher disclaim any affiliation, association, or connection with, or sponsorship or endorsement by, such owners.

**Cover image credit:** istock.com/-strizh- (semi-opaque squares; modified)

We have made every effort to trace the ownership of all copyrighted material and to secure permission from copyright holders. In the event of any question arising as to the use of any material, we will be pleased to make the necessary corrections in future printings. Thanks are due to the aforementioned authors, publishers, and agents for permission to use the materials indicated.

ISBN 978-0-76387-805-4 (print)
ISBN 978-0-76387-808-5 (digital)
Paradigm Keyboarding Online Lab: Key7e.ParadigmEducation.com

© 2018 by Paradigm Publishing, Inc.
875 Montreal Way
St. Paul, MN 55102
Email: CustomerService@ParadigmEducation.com
Website: ParadigmEducation.com

Printed in the United States of America

26 25 24 23 22 21 20 19          3 4 5 6 7 8 9 10 11

# Contents

# Preface

Keyboarding is a fundamental skill for anyone who plans to work in any type of business environment. The requirement for this skill is not limited to particular jobs. Keyboarding is required for all kinds of business settings and written communication. To be effective in communicating through email, business correspondence, and other types of documents, a person must be able to think and key simultaneously. Keyboarding is no longer a nice-to-know skill—it is now an *essential* skill.

*Paradigm Keyboarding: Sessions 1–30*, Seventh Edition, and the accompanying Online Lab provide instruction in the basic keyboarding skills needed to key alphabetic, numeric, and symbol characters on a standard keyboard. The courseware also teaches the skills needed to use a 10-key numeric keypad. No prior experience in keyboarding (or "typing") is required to use this courseware.

The emphasis of this courseware is to develop a student's keyboarding speed and accuracy as well as the ability to think and key simultaneously. After successfully completing a course that uses this textbook and the accompanying Online Lab, students will be able to do the following:

- Key straight-copy alphanumeric material using correct touch techniques at an average rate of 25 words per minute (WPM) with two or fewer errors per minute
- Key numeric copy using correct touch techniques on the 10-key numeric keypad at a rate of 25 WPM with no errors
- Compose coherent content at the keyboard at the word, sentence, and paragraph levels

## Keyboarding Program Overview

*Paradigm Keyboarding: Sessions 1–30*, Seventh Edition, and Online Lab provide a streamlined and contemporary approach to mastering lifelong keyboarding skills. In this easy-to-navigate program, students will learn how to key with speed and accuracy by watching key-reach videos, completing drills, and taking timings.

*Paradigm Keyboarding: Sessions 1–30*, Seventh Edition, includes the first 30 of the 120 sessions that comprise the Paradigm Keyboarding Series. For additional keyboarding timing practice, instruction in word processing using Microsoft® Word 2016, and instruction and practice in preparing business documents such as emails, memos, letters, reports, and manuscripts, see:

- *Paradigm Keyboarding & Applications I Using Microsoft Word 2016: Sessions 1–60*, Seventh Edition
- *Paradigm Keyboarding & Applications II Using Microsoft Word 2016: Sessions 61–120*, Seventh Edition

These titles are available at ParadigmEducation.com or by calling 800-535-6865.

*Paradigm Keyboarding: Sessions 1–30*, Seventh Edition, is divided into five units. The first three units introduce all the keys of the alphanumeric keyboard. Unit 1 introduces alphabetic keys, Unit 2 introduces top-row number keys, and Unit 3 introduces punctuation and symbol keys. Unit 4 covers the numeric keypad. Unit 5 provides instruction and practice in composing at the keyboard.

Each session is a coherent lesson with specific objectives focusing on particular keyboarding skills. Students can work at their own pace and can repeat session activities as often as needed. To keep the drill work engaging, session activities vary, but all activities are designed to help the student accomplish the session objectives. Students complete warm-up drills, new key drills, thinking drills, and timings.

Keyboarding skills are developed through practice, and the courseware provides ample practice opportunities for students. All key locations and proper finger positioning and finger reaches are clearly shown with keyboard diagrams, available in the textbook and in the Online Lab. The Online Lab delivers dynamic videos to demonstrate finger technique. Skills are continually reinforced and applied through multiple drills. Drills specifically designed to reinforce previously learned skills are identified with the repeating arrow symbol, shown at the left. In addition, the Online Lab incorporates diagnostic software that identifies keys the student is struggling with and provides additional, customized practice activities to help the student improve those key reaches. Sessions also include success tips and ergonomic tips.

 **Success Tip**

Reading numbers in groups will help you gain speed and improve accuracy. This method is also known as syllabizing numbers.

 Ergonomic Tip

Position your monitor so that the top of the screen is no higher than your eye level.

Success Tip and Ergonomic Tip feature boxes provide suggestions to help students work efficiently and effectively.

## Online Lab Features

The Paradigm Keyboarding Online Lab is a web-based keyboarding tutor and learning management system (LMS) application. Download and install the Online Lab from http://Key7e.ParadigmEducation.com. The Online Lab gives students access to their course activities from any web-connected, Windows-based computer. Instructors also have access to all student work and scores by launching and logging into the Online Lab.

All Online Lab activities are referenced in the textbook, individually numbered, and clearly identified in the left margin of the text. The activities in the Online Lab include exercises, videos, and timings.

## Exercises

To keep the drill work interesting, there are a wide variety of exercise types in the Online Lab. Students will complete activities by either referring to prompts on screen or by keying from drill lines printed in the textbook. The textbook and Online Lab provide clear directions to guide students through the learning experience. Students will not get lost!

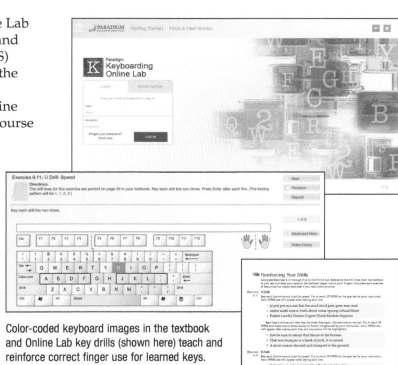

Color-coded keyboard images in the textbook and Online Lab key drills (shown here) teach and reinforce correct finger use for learned keys.

Corresponding textbook page of key drill

## Videos

Videos demonstrate correct finger positioning and finger reaches for all keys. Students can use these videos to help develop good keyboarding technique, which is essential for developing speed and accuracy.

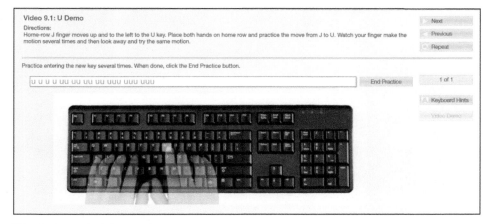

Video to demonstrate key reach

## Timings

Timings are an important tool in assessing keying proficiency, and the Online Lab provides immediate feedback on speed and accuracy for all timings. Timings begin in Session 6, with a 1-minute duration. The first 3-minute timing is introduced in Session 18, and the first 5-minute timing appears in Session 28. Instructors can adjust the minimum error and target WPM counts for timings as desired.

## Grade Book and Reports

The Online Lab includes a grade book that automatically documents the grades for all completed timings and checked document activities. Instructors can add other activities to the grade book and then enter grades for those activities. Instructors can also edit grades. All grade data may be easily exported to other learning management systems.

The Online Lab also includes reports designed to allow students and instructors to assess student progress through the courseware. The reports include the Prescriptive Analysis report, the Progress report, the Timings Performance report, and the Average Timings Performance report.

### Prescriptive Analysis Report

The Prescriptive Analysis report summarizes student success in learning each key reach and suggests reinforcement activities for keys that are difficult for the individual student.

### Progress Report

The Progress report lists all the exercises in the Online Lab and applies a check mark next to each activity for which the student has completed all the required work.

### Timings Performance Report

The Timings Performance report lists the student's best WPM score—along with the corresponding error counts—for each 1-minute, 3-minute, and 5-minute timing activity. The report can be viewed as a table or as a graph.

### Average Timings Performance Report

The Average Timings Performance report lists an average WPM rate and error count for the student for all timings taken during the entire course.

## Instructor eResources

The Keyboarding Online Lab is a web-based learning management system that lets instructors easily deliver customized keyboarding courses and efficiently communicate with enrolled students. The Online Lab includes extensive reports documenting student activity and a grade book for assigning grades and tracking student progress.

Additional instructor support is available through the Instructor eResources link in the Online Lab and includes a sample syllabus, reference material and instructional support for each session, a theory quiz, general suggestions on teaching keyboarding, as well as content for pretest and posttest timings. Students complete pretest and posttest timings in the Online Lab.

# Alphabetic Keys

**Timing**
30.5

Most of the major events in communications grew out of a series of discoveries that took place over many years. Present-day systems can be traced to many great men and women who brought together the tools of their day to meet the needs of people on the job and in the home. The basis of this technology had its start in the 1830s. In the 1830s, if you wanted to tell people things, you either had to do it in person, or write a letter and send it by means of the Post Office. The Post Office used men on horses to transport letters from one place to big cities and small towns.

One of the first events occurred in Germany when their government built a telegraph network that spanned 8,000 feet. By the next decade, the use of this device had spread to the United States. Congress funded a line that ran from Washington to Baltimore. During the same time frame, Samuel F. B. Morse finished a new telegraph device and code that came to be known as the Morse Code. The Morse Code was used for more than 100 years. It was vital for both the North and South in the Civil War.

In the next few years, more developments took place. European telegraph wires and underwater cables became widely used. While the telegraph would continue to be used for many more years, other types of technology were taking shape. Bell developed the telephone in 1875, and he and Gray filed for a patent the next year. Bell later offered to sell his patents to Western Union, but they turned him down.

The evolution of the telephone is constantly on the move. Computer telephony has entered the scene. With a web cam you can see the person you are talking to, and she/he can see you. There are no handsets. You are talking to a microphone on your computer. A small camera attached to your monitor is taking a moving picture of you that is being transmitted to the person you are talking to.

 **Ergonomic Tip**

You can make many adjustments in your own work environment at little or no cost to you or your employer.

## Ending the Session

The Online Lab automatically saved the work you completed for this session. You can continue with the next session or exit the Online Lab and continue later.

# Session 1 Home Row, Spacebar, Enter

## Session Objectives

- Access and explore the Online Lab
- Identify the home row keys
- Practice correct finger positioning for the A, S, D, F, J, K, L, and semicolon (;) keys
- Use the spacebar and Enter key appropriately
- Apply ergonomic principles to your work station
- Use correct posture when keying

## Getting Started in the Online Lab

You will be using the Online Lab application along with your textbook to complete session activities that will help you develop your keyboarding skills.

### Installing the Online Lab Software

If your computer does not already have the Online Lab application, complete the following steps to install it.

1. Connect to the Internet.
2. Launch your web browser (such as Chrome) and then go to http://key7e.paradigmeducation.com.
3. At the Paradigm Keyboarding Online Lab website, click the DOWNLOAD AND INSTALL button to download the desktop installer application.

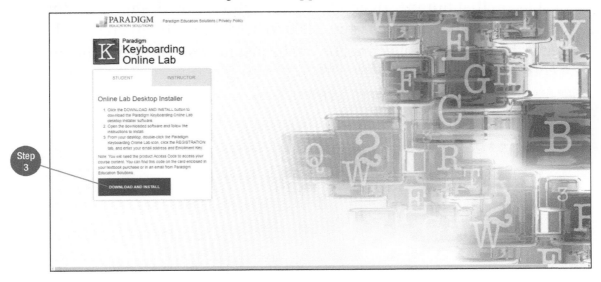

4. Click the Open, Save File, or Run button (this will vary based on your browser), open the downloaded file, and follow the instructions to install the desktop application.

## Assessing Your Speed and Accuracy

Complete Timings 30.1 through 30.5 in the Online Lab. Refer to the following paragraphs as you key.

Each timing will start as soon as you begin keying. If you finish keying the passage before the timing expires, press Enter and start keying the timing text again. Remember to press Tab at the start of each paragraph.

The Online Lab specifies the WPM and error goals. When time expires, the Online Lab will give you a WPM rate and error report for the timing and will highlight any errors you made. The results will be stored in your Timings Performance report.

Timings 30.1 and 30.2 use the same paragraph of text.

### 1-Minute Timings

**Timings 30.1–30.2**

At sunset, it is nice to enjoy dining out on a bank of a pond. Unless uninvited insects and swarms of ants invade the picnic, you will certainly unwind. As those soft night sounds encompass you, frenzied nervousness and the decisions that haunt you slip from your mind. You may enjoy napping on a nearby bench. Next, swing into action after your rest and inhale much air into your lungs. Unpack the nice lunch and munch away. Don't deny yourself this experience.

Timings 30.3 and 30.4 use the same paragraph of text.

### 3-Minute Timings

**Timings 30.3–30.4**

Simple salt and pepper shakers are very kitchy and quite simple to collect today. Lots of "fun" and very colorful pairs are available, either new or pre-owned. Bargains can be found at multi-family or group sales. Most folks try to see how many kinds they can find and buy. Some collect a mass of shakers that number over 500. People who are dedicated collectors may have shakers that number from 2,000 to 3,000 pairs. If anyone would like to begin the hobby of collecting, he or she just needs to look around and start a collection.

## Enrolling in the Online Lab

Once you have installed the Online Lab application, complete the following steps to enroll in the Online Lab for your Keyboarding course.

1 Double-click the Launch Online Lab icon on your computer desktop.

2 Click the REGISTRATION tab.

3 Enter your email address.

4 Enter the Enrollment Key given to you by your instructor for your course.

5 Click the REGISTER button.

6 Check your email for a message welcoming you to the Paradigm Keyboarding Online Lab.

7 In the body of the email message, click the CREATE AN ACCOUNT button.

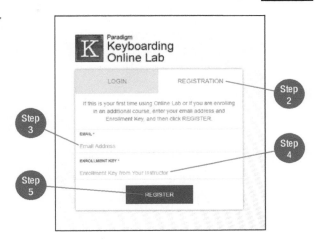

8 At the web page that displays, fill in the fields of the form to create a user account.

  a Your email address will already appear in the *Email* field.

  b Enter your first and last names.

  c Create a password at least 8 characters long, including at least one UPPERCASE letter, one number, and one special character (such as ! or #).

  d Select your time zone.

9 Click the CREATE AN ACCOUNT button.

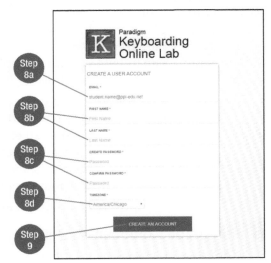

7. → Facebook

8. → dance

9. → apple

10. → water

11. → mirror

12. → television

13. → dollar bill

14. → door

15. → chair

16. → text messaging

17. → shoe

18. → building

19. → sunset

20. → clock

## General Guidelines for Writing Paragraphs

As noted in Session 28, the fourth stage in building keyboarding composition skills is to compose at the keyboard at the paragraph-response level. A paragraph is a group of related sentences—an organized and meaningful unit in a piece of writing. A paragraph contains a topic sentence and several supporting sentences. In a well-written paragraph, the sentences are organized in a logical manner and flow from one to the next. Transitional words are used to connect one sentence to another sentence, and transitional phrases are used to connect one paragraph to another paragraph.

A topic sentence expresses the main idea of a paragraph and the supporting sentences describe, explain, or further develop the topic sentence. Because most readers like to know the subject of a paragraph before reading about it, the topic sentence is usually the first sentence of a paragraph. The following is an example of a paragraph with a topic sentence as the first sentence and supporting sentences following it.

A receptionist who works in a small office has a wide variety of duties. Answering the telephone and receiving callers are primary responsibilities of any receptionist. Sometimes an employer asks a receptionist to take an important client to lunch or to contact a business customer. The correspondence in a small office varies from simple letters, memos, and emails to complicated reports, and so the receptionist handles many types of communication.

Practice composing a paragraph at the keyboard by completing Exercise 30.7 in the Online Lab.

**Exercise 30.7** Paragraph Composition Drill

Compose a paragraph about how you will use your keyboarding skills. Your paragraph should include a topic sentence and at least three supporting sentences. Start the paragraph by pressing Tab. Allow text in the paragraph to automatically wrap, correct any errors, and click the Finished button when you are done.

## Logging in to the Online Lab

Once the Online Lab application is installed on your computer and you are enrolled in the Paradigm Keyboarding course, follow these steps to log in:

1  Return to the Paradigm Keyboarding Online Lab application by clicking the Online Lab icon on the Windows taskbar or your computer desktop.

2  On the LOGIN tab, enter your email address and password.

3  Click the LOG IN button.

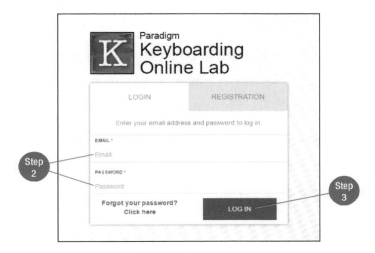

## Navigating in the Online Lab

After you log in to the Online Lab, click the course name to access the course content. The first time you access the course, a text box will appear, directing you to enter the access code you purchased for use with this course. After entering your course access code, you will see your course's activity list. You will not have to enter the access code on future visits; instead you will go directly to the course's activity list after clicking the course name.

Once logged in to your Keyboarding course, you will see a Course Menu page listing the activities in your course as well as a Navigation pane and additional resources. Figure 1.1 shows the Activity List within the Course Menu. Click an activity link to go to that activity's View page and then click the Launch button to bring up that activity.

Figure 1.1  Activity List in the Online Lab

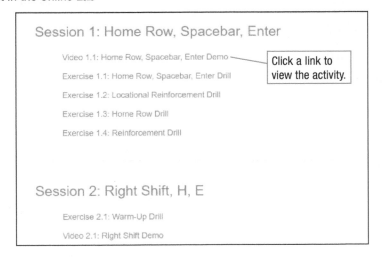

**Exercise 30.5**  Correct Word Choice Drill

Select the correct phrase from the text in parentheses in the following sentences and key each sentence using the correct words. Refer to the tables on page 156, if necessary. Before keying each sentence, key the sentence number and a period and then press Tab. Click the Finished button after keying all 15 sentences. *Hint: Do not key the parentheses or the comma within the parentheses.*

1. → (Try to, Try and) key the data without any errors.

2. → Juan went (in search for, in search of) a new printer.

3. → My book is (different from, different than) Harriet's book.

4. → I will try to (comply with, comply to) your wishes.

5. → This (kind of a, kind of) paper is easier to store.

6. → (Accept, Except) for Henry, the entire class went on the trip.

7. → Our teacher strongly (adviced, advised) us to study for the exam.

8. → There have been (fewer, less) absences this winter than last winter.

9. → We have (fewer, less) flour than we need.

10. → He is a (good, well) student.

11. → Heather doesn't feel (good, well) today.

12. → Sean plays the violin (good, well).

13. → I am angry (at, about, with) my best friend.

14. → I am angry (at, about, with) the rising cost of school.

15. → I am angry (at, about, with) Whiskers, my cat.

**Exercise 30.6**  Sentence Composition Drill

Compose a complete sentence about each of the following items. Before keying your response, key the sentence number and a period and then press Tab. If your sentence extends beyond the right margin, let word wrap work automatically. Press Enter at the end of each sentence. Be sure to correct any errors and then click the Finished button after keying all 20 sentences.

1. → hybrid car

2. → ice cream

3. → gas station

4. → bank

5. → elevator

6. → fire

*drill continues*

**Figure 1.2  Online Lab Exercise Activity Screen**

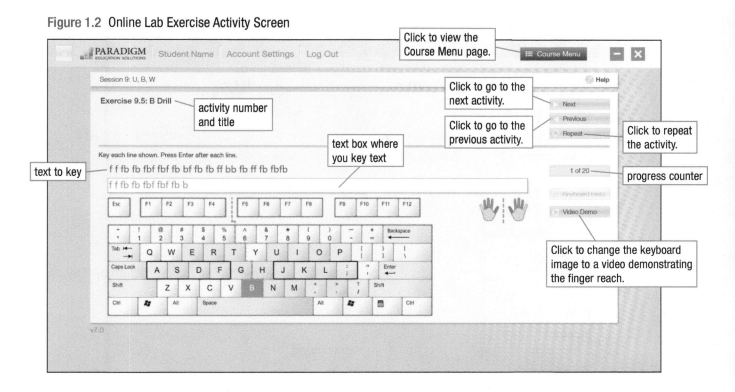

When you click the Launch button, you will see a screen similar to the one shown in Figure 1.2.

To move around the Online Lab, you can click the Next button to go to the next activity, click the Previous button to go to the previous activity, or click the Repeat button to return to the beginning of the present activity. To see the list of all activities, grouped by session (as shown in Figure 1.1), click the Course Menu button.

Directions for the activity display at the top of the activity window. If there is text for you to read as you key, it appears below the instructions. (For many activities, the text to key is in the textbook.) The insertion point (blinking vertical line) is positioned in the text box in which you will key text. Some activities are divided into more than one part. You can check how many parts of an activity you have completed by noting the progress counter on the right side of the screen.

## Introducing the Home Row Position

**Video 1.1**  When you begin to type, you will always start by placing your fingers on the same keys on the keyboard, the home row keys. As shown in the following illustration, when you are in the home row position, the fingers of your left hand are positioned over the A, S, D, and F keys, and the fingers of your right hand are positioned on the J, K, L, and semicolon (;) keys. Either your left or right thumb is positioned on the spacebar. As needed, use the little finger of your right hand to press the Enter key. Watch Video 1.1 in the Online Lab and practice the home row position. *Note: Your keyboard may appear somewhat different than the one illustrated in this courseware.*

**2** Use the correct phrase. The following are commonly misused phrases.

| Correct | Incorrect | Correct | Incorrect |
|---|---|---|---|
| acquitted of | acquitted from | in search of | in search for |
| aim to prove | aim at proving | kind of (+ noun) | kind of a (+ noun) |
| can't help feeling | can't help but feel | different from | different than |
| comply with | comply to | try to | try and |
| independent of | independent from | home in | hone in |

**3** Use the correct word. The following are commonly misused words.

| | | |
|---|---|---|
| angry at<br>*(things and animals)* | angry with<br>*(people)* | angry about<br>*(occasions or situations)* |
| there<br>*a place* | their<br>*possession* | they're<br>*contraction of they are* |
| accept<br>*to take or receive* | except<br>*to leave out; aside from* | |
| advice<br>*a recommendation* | advise<br>*to recommend* | |
| affect<br>*to produce an effect* | effect<br>*a result* | |
| biannual<br>*twice a year* | biennial<br>*once every two years* | |
| council<br>*a governing body* | counsel<br>*to give advice* | |
| ensure<br>*to make sure* | insure<br>*to provide insurance* | |
| fewer<br>*(use with nouns that can<br>  be counted: fewer apples)* | less<br>*(use with nouns that cannot<br>  be counted: less noise)* | |
| good<br>*modifies a noun or pronoun* | well<br>*modifies a verb or adverb* | |

**Exercise** Descriptive Sentences Drill
**30.4**

Drawing from your experience and observations, think of descriptive words or phrases to make the following five sentences more interesting. Key the sentence number and a period, press Tab, and then key your revised sentence. If your sentence extends beyond the right margin, let word wrap work automatically. At the end of each sentence, press Enter and continue with the next sentence. Click the Finished button after keying all five sentences.

1.→ The last book I read was good.

2.→ Today is a nice day.

3.→ My favorite sport is fun.

4.→ My favorite color is a nice color.

5.→ My best friend is nice.

**Exercises
1.1–1.2**  Practice using the home row keys, spacebar, and Enter key by completing the drills in Exercises 1.1–1.2 in the Online Lab. All of the drill work you do in the lab will be saved automatically.

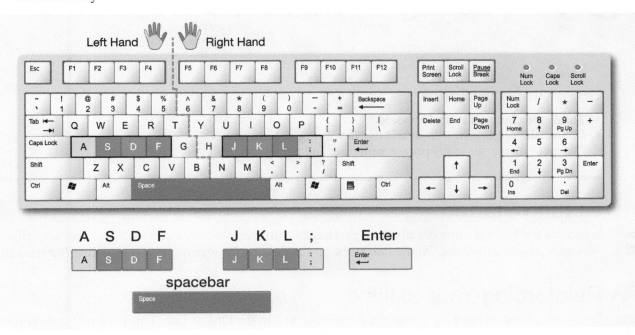

##  Reinforcing Your Skills

You will continue to practice using the home row keys, spacebar, and Enter key in the following drills. Type the following drill lines for Exercises 1.3 and 1.4 in the Online Lab.

### 🎓 Success Tip

Whether working from the screen or the text, keep your eyes on the copy (the source text you're typing from), not on your fingers. This will help you build speed.

## Session 30 Composing Sentences and Paragraphs at the Keyboard

### Session Objectives

- **Think and compose at the keyboard**
- **Choose the correct word form and use in varying circumstances**
- **Compose responses at the phrase, sentence, and paragraph level**

### Getting Started

**Exercise 30.1** If you are continuing immediately from Session 29, you may skip the Exercise 30.1 warm-up drill. However, if you exited the Online Lab at the end of Session 29, warm up by completing Exercise 30.1.

### Reinforcing Your Skills

**Exercises 30.2–30.3** Begin your session work by completing Exercise 30.2 in the Online Lab. This drill will give you the opportunity to further reinforce your keyboarding skills by providing practice using the numeric keypad and keying sentences. Then complete Exercise 30.3, a timed short drill.

### Composing at the Keyboard

In Session 29, you worked on keying responses that were word phrases and sentences. In this session, you will focus on developing your composition skills at the sentence-response and paragraph-response levels.

#### General Guidelines for Correct Word Use

A common problem a writer faces is choosing the correct word to convey a certain thought or idea to the reader. Writing must be precise. Vague words or misuse of words may produce a response from readers that differs from the author's intended meaning. The following are guidelines to help you choose the correct word.

1 Use nouns and descriptive adjectives, adverbs, and phrases that have a precise meaning. Be specific when you write. Do not use vague or abstract words such as *nice*, *good*, *bad*, *thing*, and *work* because they do not give the reader much information. Read each of the following examples and notice the differences.

| | |
|---|---|
| *Vague:* | The lecture was good, and I learned a lot. |
| *Better:* | The lecture solved two problems for me. I learned how to balance a checkbook and how to calculate interest. |
| *Vague:* | a nice color |
| *Better:* | an emerald green, a vivid scarlet, a deep black |
| *Vague:* | he said |
| *Better:* | he shouted defiantly, he muttered, he demanded, he whispered |

**Exercise
1.3**

## Home Row Drill

- Key each line once. Do not key the number at the beginning of each line.
- Press the Enter key quickly at the end of each line.
- Keep your eyes on the drill lines in the textbook as you key.
- Repeat the exercise if you need more practice.

1 aaa sss ddd fff jjj kkk lll ;;; sd kl ;

2 aa ss dd ff jj kk ll ;; asdf jkl; af j;

3 a s d f j k l ; aa ss dd ff jj kk ll ;;

4 a ad a ad add add adds adds a ad add ad

5 a as as a ask ask asks asks a all all a

6 ad add as ask a; a; as adds asks a;; ad

7 fads fads fall fall falls falls fad fad

8 lass lass lad lad lads dad dads ask ask

9 falls flask alas fads dads asks all sad

**Exercise
1.4**

## Reinforcement Drill

Key the following drill lines. Press the Enter key quickly after each line. Your words per minute (WPM) rate will appear after keying each line. (In keyboarding, one word equals five keystrokes. Each character [number, letter, or punctuation mark], space, and return [Enter] is counted as a keystroke.)

1 all all

2 sad sad dad dad

3 fad fad alas alas

4 fall fall lad lad add add

5 a all all a alas alas a as ad add ask a

6 ask ask asks asks all all alas alas all

7 ad add as ask all alas adds asks all ad

8 dad dad dads dads sad sad fad fad fads

9 flak flak flask flask lad lad lads lads

 **Ergonomic Tip**

Sit upright in your seat to eliminate lower back pain and strain. Correct posture for keyboarding is illustrated in Figure 1.3.

**Timing
29.5**

Education has become a lifelong process. No longer can we say that a person's formal schooling will last her a lifetime. Business spends almost as much for training programs as is spent for our public school system. The average age of students in schools offering programs above the high school level is on the rise.

Adult learners enter school programs with needs and wants that differ from the requirements of traditional students. They are goal oriented. They are looking for skills and knowledge that will help them keep a job, prepare for a new job, or advance to a higher-level job. Adults don't want to waste time in reaching new skills; they want to spend their time on those things that relate to their goals.

Teachers and trainers of adult learners are faced with a tough task. In most cases, they must narrow the focus of their programs to meet the needs of the learners. Courses must be designed that draw upon the learners' skills and knowledge. To design a good program, you must assess what the learners know and what their goals are.

The next step in the process is to design a performance outcome that shows that the person can demonstrate a mastery of what was presented in the course. Once the outcome has been set, the instructor can choose teaching methods, course length, texts needed, and program content. Problem-solving, learning by doing, and case studies are methods of teaching that help adult students.

 **Ergonomic Tip**

Sit up straight, drop your shoulders back, and let your arms and hands hang loosely. This takes the strain off your back and allows your lungs and other organs to function correctly.

## Ending the Session

The Online Lab automatically saved the work you completed for this session. You can continue with the next session or exit the Online Lab and continue later.

Figure 1.3 Correct Keyboarding Posture

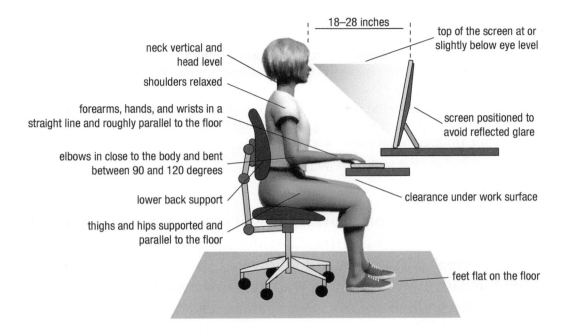

## Ending the Session

The Online Lab automatically saved the work you completed for this session. You can continue with the next session or exit the Online Lab and continue later. Instructions for completing these actions follow and are also available in the Online Lab.

### Continuing with the Next Session

You can continue to the next session in the Online Lab by clicking the Next button twice. This will take you to Video 2.1. *Note: You may skip Exercise 2.1, a warm-up drill, because by completing Session 1 you are already warmed up*.

### Exiting the Online Lab

To exit the Online Lab, simply click the Close (×) button in the upper right corner of your screen.

## Assessing Your Speed and Accuracy

Complete Timings 29.1 through 29.5 in the Online Lab. Refer to the following timing text as you key Timings.

Each timing will start as soon as you begin keying. Remember to press Tab at the start of each paragraph. If you finish keying the passage before time expires, press Enter and start keying the timing text again.

The Online Lab specifies the WPM and error goals. When time expires, the Online Lab will give you a WPM rate and error report for the timing and will highlight any errors you made. The results will be stored in your Timings Performance Report.

Timings 29.1 and 29.2 use the same paragraph of text.

### 1-Minute Timings

**Timings 29.1–29.2**

The news on the network newscast might spawn a winning wealth of followers. If the newscaster can draw a wider range of viewers, the rewards are power and wealth. Watchers and followers of a witty newscaster are won when the daily news is written well. It is not a waste to rewrite the worst of interviews when witless words can wreck a well-planned show or review. They who dawdle in the newsroom will not work or write very long. Their reward will be awful reviews.

Timings 29.3 and 29.4 use the same paragraph of text.

### 3-Minute Timings

**Timings 29.3–29.4**

Taking photos with a good camera can be fun. A cheap brand does not work well. Though most cell phones now take good photos with ease, a real camera gives you more control. Most photo equipment has some method of setting a variety of focal lengths. A focal length setting of 35 mm gives a wider picture angle, and it can be used for group portraits or photos of landscapes. Most folks like good pictures of pretty green hills with blue lakes. A focal length setting of 70 mm has a narrow angle for making a portrait or taking a good photo of a good scene or object that is far away. Using the zoom lens requires some practice before a picture can be a work of art.

# Session 2  Right Shift, H, E

## Session Objectives

- **Identify the Shift, H, and E keys**
- **Practice correct finger positioning for the right Shift, H, and E keys**
- **Learn how to key uppercase letters**
- **Use words per minute (WPM) rate to set speed goals**
- **Practice WPM rate for the right Shift, H, and E keys**

## Getting Started

**Exercise 2.1**

If you exited the Online Lab at the end of Session 1, complete the following steps:

1 At the Windows desktop on your computer screen, double-click the Launch Online Lab icon on your desktop. *Note: If the computer you are using for this session doesn't have a Launch Online Lab icon, see the instructions on page 2 for installing the Online Lab application, or if you are in a school computer lab, contact your instructor.*

2 Key your email address and password.

3 Click the LOG IN button.

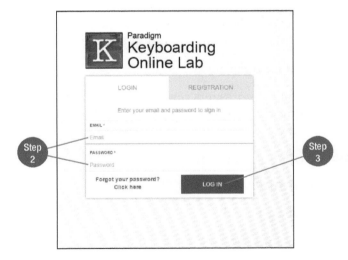

4 At the Course Menu page, click <u>Exercise 2.1: Warm-Up Drill</u>.

5 Warm up by completing Exercise 2.1.

*steps continue*

6. → If I pass this test, I _____.

7. → If I finish early, I _____.

8. → If I get the job, I _____.

9. → If the price is right, I _____.

10. → If the beach is crowded, I _____.

11. → I do not like to use Twitter because _____.

12. → I do not study at the library because _____.

13. → I do obey the speed limit because _____.

14. → I do like math because _____.

15. → I do play sports because _____.

16. → A hammer is used to _____.

17. → A lawn mower is used to _____.

18. → Scissors are used to _____.

19. → A blog is used to_____.

20. → An eraser is used to _____.

**Exercise 29.7**  Sentences Drill

Read each sentence and compose a full sentence that answers each question. Before each sentence answer, key the question number, a period, and press Tab. (Do not type the question itself.) For example, in response to the first question, you might key the following:

> 1. → **A police officer enforces laws.**

In the previous example, the → represents pressing the Tab key. Try to not hesitate and to key your sentence answer as quickly as possible after reading each question. Click the Finished button after keying all 10 sentences.

1 What does a police officer do?

2 What does a plumber do?

3 What does a firefighter do?

4 What does a lawyer do?

5 What does a teacher do?

6 What does an auto mechanic do?

7 What does YouTube have to offer the public?

8 What does a dentist do?

9 What does an accountant do?

10 What does a chef do?

**6** Follow the directions at the top of your screen. When you are finished warming up, click the Next button.

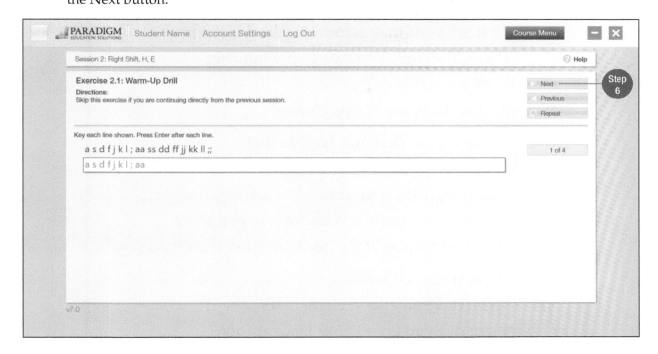

## Introducing the Right Shift, H, and E Keys

**Videos 2.1–2.3** The locations of the right Shift, H, and E keys are shown in the following diagram. In this and subsequent keyboard diagrams, new keys are shown in darker colors and previously introduced keys are shown in lighter colors. *Note: The right Shift key is used to make uppercase letters that are keyed with the left hand.* Watch Videos 2.1 through 2.3 and practice using these new keys.

**Exercises 2.2–2.5** Complete Exercises 2.2 through 2.5 to learn these new keys. When keying the drill lines, follow the instruction prompts in the Online Lab.

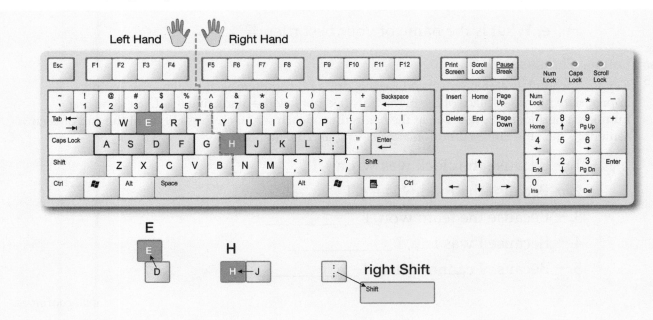

1.→ a. What is the name of a town and state or province that you would like to visit?
→ b. What are your instructor's first and last names?
→ c. What is the president's or prime minister's last name?
→ d. What is the title of this book?
→ e. What is the name of this course?

2.→ a. What are your first and last names?
→ b. What is your street address?
→ c. What is the title of your favorite song?
→ d. What is the name of the last movie you saw?
→ e. What is the name of the last television show you saw?

3.→ a. Where were you born?
→ b. Where did you attend elementary school?
→ c. Where did you go on your last vacation?
→ d. Where are you going after class today?
→ e. Where will you be tomorrow at this time?

4.→ a. What are your favorite sports?
→ b. What are your favorite colors?
→ c. What will you be doing five years from now?
→ d. What is the name of your favorite class?
→ e. What is the name of your best friend?

**Exercise 29.6** Longer Phrases Drill

Key the incomplete statements listed for this drill and complete each sentence by keying an appropriate phrase in place of the blank line. (Do not key the blank line itself.) Key the line number, a period, and press Tab at the beginning of each sentence. Press Enter at the end of each sentence. Click the Finished button after keying all 20 sentences.

1.→ Because the clock was wrong, I _____.
2.→ Because the road was icy, I _____.
3.→ Because the team won, I _____.
4.→ Because I was late, I _____.
5.→ Because I cannot drive, I _____.

*drill continues*

##  Reinforcing Your Skills

Complete Exercises 2.6 through 2.9 in the Online Lab. Reference the drill lines from the textbook as you key and keep your eyes on the textbook pages, not on your fingers. Key each line once and press the Enter key quickly at the end of each line. Complete each exercise at least once, but repeat exercises if you need more practice.

> 🎓 **Success Tip**
>
> Your wrists should hover above the keyboard. Do not rest them while you key.

**Exercise 2.6** Right Shift Drill

Key each drill line once. Press Enter after each line.

1 Ad All Asks Adds Alas All Ask As Add Ad

2 Fad fad Falls falls Fall fall Fads fads

3 Sad All Asks Dads Fads Alas Flask Falls

**Exercise 2.7** H Drill

Key each drill line once. Press Enter after each line.

1 jh hall hall hall sash sash has sash hash

2 half half half lash lash lash half lash

3 Dads sash Falls Shall Shall Flash Flash

**Exercise 2.8** E Drill

Key lines 1 and 2 for speed. Key each line twice. In other words, key line 1, press Enter, key line 1 a second time, and then press Enter. Continue this pattern when you key line 2. Try to make your fingers go faster as you key each line a second time.

1 deal dead deaf fade led lead lease lake

2 she she ale ale elf elf elk elk heal heal fake fake

Key lines 3–5 once and then key the three lines again. In other words, key lines 3, 4, and 5 and then key lines 3, 4, and 5 again. Remember to press Enter after each line. As you key these lines, slow down a bit and concentrate on control.

3 deal deal ease ease else else desk desk fell fell

4 fade fade feel feel dead dead head head heal heal

5 Elk Elk Else Ease Ed Elf Else Ease Ed Ed

## Session 29    Composing Phrases and Sentences at the Keyboard

### Session Objectives

- **Think and compose at the keyboard**
- **Compose responses at the phrase and sentence level**

---

### Getting Started

**Exercise 29.1**   If you are continuing immediately from Session 28, you may skip the Exercise 29.1 warm-up drill. However, if you exited the Online Lab at the end of Session 28, warm up by completing Exercise 29.1.

### Reinforcing Your Skills

**Exercises 29.2–29.4**   Begin your session work by completing Exercises 29.2 and 29.3 in the Online Lab. These drills will give you the opportunity to further reinforce your keyboarding skills by providing practice using the numeric keypad and keying sentences. Exercise 29.4 is a timed short drill. As described in Session 28, in timed short drills you (1) indicate your goal of working to improve speed or accuracy; (2) set the drill duration at 15 seconds, 30 seconds, or 60 seconds; and (3) identify your personal WPM goal for the timing. Complete each exercise at least once, but repeat exercises if you want to improve your WPM rate and accuracy.

### Composing Phrases at the Keyboard

In Session 28, you worked on single-word responses. In this session, you will focus on developing your phrase-response and sentence-response keyboarding skills.

**Exercise 29.5**   **Short Phrases Drill**

For the first question in each group, key the question number followed by a period, press Tab (indicated with a → in the drill line), key a., press the spacebar once, and then key the question. Following the question, press the spacebar once, key your answer in the format of a short answer or phrase, and then press Enter. For each of the remaining questions, press Tab, key the question letter followed by a period and a space, key the question followed by a space, type your answer, and then press Enter.

Think about each question as you key the question text, and try to key your answer as quickly as possible after striking the question mark and spacebar at the end of the question. Click the Finished button after keying all four sets of questions and responses.

## Exercise 2.9 Reinforcement Drill

Key the following drill lines once. Press Enter after each line. Your words per minute (WPM) rate will appear after keying each line. Repeat this exercise if you would like more practice.

1 lad lad lads lads Flak Flak Flask Flask
2 fall hall alas dash half
3 flash flash shall shall
4 half half

5 Sad Dad Add Ask Fad Salad Flak Dads All
6 Dads Ask lad Ask dad lads lass lass Add
7 jh has had has had has had has had lash
8 ha has ash Ash Ash had ash ash hall Flash

9 eel deed eel she see she see ale elf ale fee
10 ease deal ease deal else desk else desk fell
11 fade feel fade feel dead head dead head heal
12 Else Elk Ease Ed Elf Else Ease Ed Elf Ed

### Ergonomic Tip

To avoid strain or potential long-term pain, just tap the keys lightly when keying. Pressing the keys too hard will slow you down and cause unnecessary hand fatigue.

## Ending the Session

The Online Lab automatically saved the work you completed for this session. You can continue with the next session or exit the Online Lab and continue later. If you need to review the procedures for continuing to the next session or exiting the Online Lab, refer back to Session 1, page 8.

Timing 28.5 is the first 5-minute timing. It is intended to help you build endurance for keying longer documents.

### 5-Minute Timing

**Timing 28.5**

The most important piece of furniture in an office is the chair. Workers will spend most of their days doing their work while seated. If people are uncomfortable, they will not be as productive as they could be with the right chair. It has been stated that a person's productivity will increase 15 to 20 percent when using a chair that fits his or her body.

There are several features to look for in selecting a chair to be used in an office setting. First, make sure it has a five-point base so that it won't tip over. Next, make sure that the seat adjusts upward and downward to fit the person using it. The backrest must be adjustable up and down so that it supports the worker's back. The front of the chair must have a "waterfall," or downward-curved cushion, so that there is no pressure behind the knees while the worker is seated.

Any adjustments to be made to chair height, back support, or tilt must be easy to do. There are chairs on the market that adjust as the person sits down; no manual adjustments need to be made. Another important part of a chair is the covering. Some coverings are warm (because they don't breathe). Chairs can be purchased with arms that drop so that the chair can be moved closer to the desk.

 **Ergonomic Tip**

Take small breaks of at least 10 seconds every 30 minutes to stretch. Short breaks like this will help you relax and relieve tension.

## Ending the Session

The Online Lab automatically saved the work you completed for this session. You can continue with the next session or exit the Online Lab and continue later.

## Session 3 — Period, T, Comma, Caps Lock

# Session 3 · Period, T, Comma, Caps Lock

## Session Objectives

- Identify the period (.), T, comma (,), and Caps Lock keys
- Practice correct finger positioning for the period (.), T, comma (,), and Caps Lock keys
- Create simple responses to statements or questions while keying
- Improve keyboarding speed

## Getting Started

**Exercise 3.1**  If you are continuing immediately from Session 2, you may skip the Exercise 3.1 warm-up drill. However, if you exited the Online Lab at the end of Session 2, warm up by completing Exercise 3.1. Refer to page 9 of Session 2 for instructions on logging on to the Online Lab and navigating to the appropriate exercise.

## Introducing the Period, T, Comma, and Caps Lock Keys

**Videos 3.1–3.4**  The locations of the period (.), T, comma (,), and Caps Lock keys are shown in the following diagram. Watch Videos 3.1 through 3.4 and practice using these new keys.

**Exercises 3.2–3.6**  Complete Exercises 3.2 through 3.5 to learn these new keys. Also complete the thinking drill, Exercise 3.6. When keying the drill lines, follow the instruction prompts in the Online Lab.

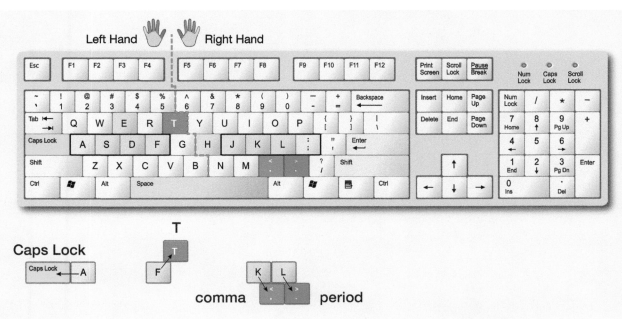

As has been the case in all previous timings, each timing will begin as soon as you begin keying. Remember to press Tab at the beginning of a paragraph. If you finish keying the passage of text before time expires, press Enter and start keying the passage again.

When time expires, the Online Lab will give you a WPM rate and error report for the timing and will highlight any errors you made. The results will be stored in your Timings Performance Report.

Timings 28.1 and 28.2 use the same paragraph of text.

### 1-Minute Timings

**Timings 28.1–28.2**

Long ago, pilgrims loved to indulge in blunt folklore. Tales, sometimes false, were told with glee daily. One old tale included a blazing clash of sailors in balky sailboats on a bottomless lake. The last sailor alive was a lad that was blind. As he lay clinging to a slim balsa log in slimy silt and filth, the leader's falcon led help to him. Balmy days followed as the lad's leg healed slowly and the salves applied to his eyes let the light in.

Timings 28.3 and 28.4 use the same paragraph of text.

### 3-Minute Timings

**Timings 28.3–28.4**

To change a US unit of measure to a metric unit of measure takes some practice and knowledge. To change back and forth, a table of metric measures and US units of measures is great to have at hand. For instance, 1 mile is equal to a metric measurement of 1.6 kilometers (or km, for short). One yard is about the same as a metric measure of 0.9 meters. One can change a large metric unit to a smaller one by moving the decimal point one place to the left.

# Reinforcing Your Skills

Complete Exercises 3.7 through 3.12 in the Online Lab. Reference the drill lines from the textbook as you key and keep your eyes on the textbook pages, not on your fingers. Complete each exercise at least once, but repeat exercises if you need more practice.

 **Success Tip**

Whether working from the screen or the text, keep your eyes on the source text, not on your fingers. This will help you build speed.

**Exercise 3.7**  Period Drill

Key each drill line once. Press the spacebar only once after the period at the end of a sentence. If a period ends a line, press Enter immediately; do not press the spacebar first.

1  All lads shall dash. A lad shall fall.

2  Ask a sad lad. Sad lads fall. Ask Al.

3  Add Jake as last dads. Hats stall a test.

**Exercise 3.8**  T Drill

Key each drill line once. Press Enter after each line.

1  ft at hat hats sat sat tall tall data data

2  fast fast slat slat halt halt last last fat fat

3  test eat the these that steed staff sat set heat

**Exercise 3.9**  Comma Drill

Key each drill line once. Do not insert a space before a comma. Be sure to insert one space after each comma. Press Enter after each line.

1  That tall, fat, fast lad shall ask Dad.

2  A flat, half lath falls; all lads halt.

3  Fasted at Tea Lake, left felt hats, sat aft safe seat.

**Exercise 3.10**  Caps Lock Drill

Key each drill line once. Remember that the home row A finger reaches to press the Caps Lock key to type a series of words in uppercase. Press the Caps Lock key again to return to lowercase letters. Press Enter after each line.

1  TALK AT A FAST LAD; a sad lad has a fall.

2  Dad halts a tall lad. A SAD LAD HALTS.

3  JED HAD LEAD FEET. Lathe at SHADE DEAD.

**Exercise 3.11**  Speed Drill

Your mind controls your fingers, so think *speed*. After you practice setting your mental goal several times, you should find that your mind eventually controls your fingers automatically.

**Exercise 28.7** Word-Response Drill: Opposites

In this drill, rather than keying the word shown, key a word with the opposite meaning. For example, if the word shown was wet, you would likely key dry.

Press Tab before each letter and press Enter immediately after each word. Click the Finished button after keying both sets of words.

1.→ a. day
 → b. salt
 → c. mother
 → d. uncle
 → e. grandmother
 → f. rich
 → g. war
 → h. young
 → i. love
 → j. hot

2.→ a. clean
 → b. male
 → c. minus
 → d. seldom
 → e. floor
 → f. stop
 → g. no
 → h. winter
 → i. sick
 → j. true

## Assessing Your Speed and Accuracy

When you take the timings, you will want to decide if your personal goal is to improve either your speed or your accuracy. It is important to concentrate on only one goal at a time. Your goal will probably change daily—or even during a particular class period. Timings throughout the Online Lab provide WPM and accuracy goals for you to work toward. *Note: With this session, the default WPM goals for 1-minute and 3-minute timings have been increased by 5 WPM in the Online Lab. However, your instructor may have customized these goals.* Continue striving to make two or fewer errors per minute in all of the timings.

Complete Timings 28.1 through 28.3 in the Online Lab. Refer to the following paragraphs from the textbook as you key.

Key each line twice. Press Enter after each line. (Key the lines in the order of 1, 1, 2, 2, 3, 3.) Try to make your fingers go faster as you key each line a second time.

1 Talk at a fast lad; a sad lad has a hat.

2 A lad talks; the dad talks; a dad talks.

3 Dad halts the sad lad. A sad lad halts.

**Exercise 3.12** Reinforcement Drill

Key the following drill lines once. Press Enter after each line. Your words per minute (WPM) rate will appear after keying each line. Repeat this exercise if you are hesitating while you key the drill lines.

1 The lads dash. A dad asks the lads.

2 Feds dash. Dads dash. Dads ask the sad lads.

3 Ask Al. Sad lads halt. Ask a sad lad.

4 data data data slat slat slat jet jet jet

5 that that that task task task talk talk talk

6 salt salt salt flat flat flat lath lath lath

7 A flat atlas; a flat hat; a flat flask.

8 A half a flask; a half lath; half a slat.

9 A sad lad halts. Dale halts a fat lad.

10 A sad lad has a hat. Talk at a fast lad.

11 A half lath; half a flask; half a slat.

12 The fat lads talked fast. A dad talks fast.

13 Dash, Al, flat, half, lath, head, heat,

14 A fat, sad, flat, hall shaft has the lead.

15 Dale asked Al. Dad asked the lads.

 **Ergonomic Tip**

The top of the computer screen should be at eye level or slightly below. If you wear bifocal or multifocal glasses, however, the screen should be low enough so that you do not have to tip your head up to read it. You can adjust your monitor or chair to the correct position.

## Ending the Session

The Online Lab automatically saved the work you completed for this session. You can continue with the next session or exit the Online Lab and continue later. If you need to review the procedures for continuing to the next session or exiting the Online Lab, refer back to Session 1, page 8.

**Exercise**
**28.6**

Word-Response Drill: Which One?

Key the questions in this drill and, at the end of each line, key appropriate one-word answers. Follow the same procedure as you did for Exercise 28.5; press Tab before each question letter, key the question letter followed by a period and a space, key the question followed by a space, key your answer, and then press Enter. Try not to hesitate when keying your answer to each question. Click the Finished button after keying all four sets of questions and responses.

1.→ a. Would you rather ski or swim?
→ b. Would you rather drive or ride?
→ c. Would you rather eat or cook?
→ d. Would you rather walk or run?
→ e. Would you rather hike or bike?

2.→ a. Are you a female or a male?
→ b. Are you right- or left-handed?
→ c. Is the instructor of this class male or female?
→ d. Would you rather drink milk or tea?
→ e. Would you rather dance or read?

3.→ a. Would you rather dance or sing?
→ b. Would you rather eat fish or steak?
→ c. Would you rather write or read?
→ d. Would you rather study or play?
→ e. Would you rather own a dog or a cat?

4.→ a. Do you like summer or winter better?
→ b. Would you rather be short or tall?
→ c. Would you rather be dirty or clean?
→ d. Would you rather win or lose?
→ e. Would you rather run or walk?

## Session 4 — N, Left Shift, Colon

### Session Objectives

- **Identify the N, left Shift, and colon (:) keys**
- **Practice correct finger positioning for the N, left Shift, and colon (:) keys**
- **Use correct technique to make uppercase letters and colons**
- **Use 10-second timings to build keyboarding speed**
- **Employ critical thinking when keyboarding**

### Getting Started

**Exercise 4.1** If you are continuing immediately from Session 3, you may skip the Exercise 4.1 warm-up drill. However, if you exited the Online Lab at the end of Session 3, warm up by completing Exercise 4.1. Refer to page 9 of Session 2 for instructions on logging on to the Online Lab and navigating to the appropriate exercise.

### Introducing the N, Left Shift, and Colon Keys

**Videos 4.1–4.2** The locations of the N, left Shift, and colon (:) keys are shown in the following diagram. Watch Videos 4.1 and 4.2 and practice using these new keys.

**Exercises 4.2–4.8** Complete Exercises 4.2 through 4.7 to learn these new keys. Also complete the thinking drill, Exercise 4.8. When keying the drill lines, follow the instruction prompts in the Online Lab.

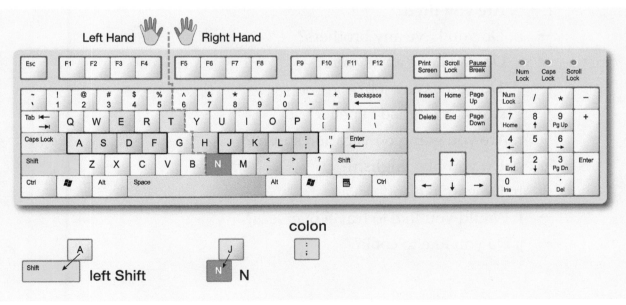

You will work on developing your keyboarding skill at the word-response level in Exercises 28.5 through 28.7 in the Online Lab. Carefully read the drill instructions that accompany each exercise in the textbook. Do not watch your fingers as you key.

**Exercise 28.5**  **Word-Response Drill: Yes or No**

For the first question in each group, key the question number followed by a period, press Tab (indicated with a → in the drill line), key a., press the spacebar once, and then key the question. Following the question, press the spacebar once, key your answer (yes, no, or not sure), and then press Enter. For each of the remaining questions, press Tab, key the question letter followed by a period and a space, key the question followed by a space, key your answer, and then press Enter.

Think about each question as you key the question text, and try to key your answer as quickly as possible after striking the question mark and spacebar at the end of the question. Click the Finished button after keying both sets of questions and responses.

1.→ a. Do you like the weather today?
→ b. Do you use Facebook?
→ c. Are you hungry?
→ d. Do you read the newspaper?
→ e. Would you like to go into politics?
→ f. Do you participate in any sport?
→ g. Do you like animals?
→ h. Do you text message?
→ i. Do you read the newspaper online?
→ j. Do you watch television every day?

2.→ a. Are you tired?
→ b. Do you have any brothers?
→ c. Do you have any sisters?
→ d. Do you have a job?
→ e. Are you a "good" speller?
→ f. Are you going on vacation soon?
→ g. Do you like English?
→ h. Do you like coffee?
→ i. Would you like to travel overseas?
→ j. Do you like to cook?

 Reinforcing Your Skills

Complete Exercises 4.9 through 4.11 in the Online Lab. Reference the drill lines from the textbook as you key and keep your eyes on the textbook pages, not on your fingers.

To increase your keyboarding skills, you must key without watching your fingers. Concentrate on keeping your eyes on the source text, whether it is on the screen or in the textbook. When keying at a controlled rate or for accuracy, concentrate on making the correct reaches. When pushing for speed, concentrate on making your fingers move faster.

Complete each exercise at least once, but repeat exercises if you need more practice.

> **Success Tip**
>
> Think *speed* as you key each line. Gain confidence as you keep your eyes on the source text.

**Exercise 4.9**  **N Drill**

Key each line twice (in the order of 1, 1, 2, 2). Push for speed and remember to press Enter at the end of each line.

1 an an and and land land sand sand

2 then then than than thank thank

Key lines 3–5 once and then key the three lines again. (Key the lines in the order of 1, 2, 3, 1, 2, 3.) Concentrate on control.

3 Jan shall hand a sad lad an atlas fast.

4 Hal shall thank that tall and lank lad.

5 Hats and sandals shall stand as fads.

**Exercise 4.10**  **Left Shift and Colon Drill**

Pressing Shift and the semicolon (;) key produces a colon (:). Practice using these keys by keying the following drill lines once. (Drill lines in this course have varied spacing for training purposes. When keying documents in a word processing program, insert one space after a colon or semicolon that follows a word.)

1 jJ kK lL ;: Jj Kk Ll ;: JL; jK lL ;:;: KL: hH:

2 Had; Lad; Has; Lass; Half: Lads: Hall: Jade:

3 Lass Lad Lads Head: Halt: Lead: Lads: Jet:

# Session
# 28

# Composing Words at the Keyboard

## Session Objectives

- **Think and compose at the keyboard**
- **Compose responses at the word level**

## Getting Started

**Exercise 28.1**  If you are continuing immediately from Session 27, you may skip the Exercise 28.1 warm-up drill. However, if you exited the Online Lab at the end of Session 27, warm up by completing Exercise 28.1.

## Reinforcing Your Skills

**Exercises 28.2–28.4**  Begin your session work by completing Exercises 28.2 and 28.3 in the Online Lab. These drills will give you the opportunity to further reinforce your keyboarding skills by providing practice using the numeric keypad and keying sentences.

Exercise 28.4 is a timed short drill. In this drill, you (1) indicate if your goal is to improve speed or accuracy; (2) set the drill duration at 15 seconds, 30 seconds, or 60 seconds; and (3) identify your personal WPM goal for the timing. Complete each exercise at least once, but repeat exercises if you want to improve your WPM rate or accuracy. It is important that you select appropriate goals each time and that you focus intently on meeting those goals.

Timed short drills, which you will encounter in many of the remaining sessions in this book, are very effective in developing speed and accuracy. They are particularly useful for students whose skills have plateaued. That is, if your WPM rate has not improved during the last several sessions, you can select a short duration time and a WPM rate slightly greater than what you have recently achieved. Repeat the drill until you attain your new WPM goal. Likewise, you can improve accuracy by selecting an error goal that is superior (that is, a lower value) to what you have recently achieved. Repeat the drill until you attain your new error goal.

## Composing at the Keyboard

In this session, you will learn to think and compose at the keyboard, which will assist you in using a computer efficiently. The four stages in building composition skills are as follows:

1 Developing skill at the *word*-response level. That is, responding to questions with a single-word answer.

2 Developing skill at the *phrase*-response level.

3 Developing skill at the *sentence*-response level.

4 Developing skill at the *paragraph*-response level.

**Exercise**  Reinforcement Drill
4.11

Key the following drill lines once. Press Enter after each line. Your WPM rate will appear after keying each line. Try to reach 25 WPM (or the goal set by your instructor). Repeat this exercise to improve your speed.

1. land land than than flank flank tan tan slant slant
2. thank thank nest nest and Dan Dan Landers Landers
3. A slanted shaft lands and halts that task.

4. As a fad, hats and sandals shall stand the sand.
5. Del and Dana shall stand and talk last.
6. flash: flash; half: half; sand: sand; hand: hand;

7. Jean shall sell the saddle, jeans, and seashells.
8. Handle the fat kettle that leaks; taste the tea.
9. The fat hen left the lake. She landed at a nest.
10. Dad and the ten lads halted a theft. Dad felt tense.

 **Ergonomic Tip**
Use only finger movements—not wrist movements—to press the keys.

## Ending the Session

The Online Lab automatically saved the work you completed for this session. You can continue with the next session or exit the Online Lab and continue later. If you need to review the procedures for continuing to the next session or exiting the Online Lab, refer back to Session 1, page 8.

# Unit 5

# Thinking and Composing at the Keyboard

**Session 28**
Composing Words at the Keyboard

**Session 29**
Composing Phrases and Sentences at the Keyboard

**Session 30**
Composing Sentences and Paragraphs at the Keyboard

## Session 5

# I, G, Tab, Word Wrap

## Session Objectives

- **Identify the I, G, and Tab keys**
- **Practice correct finger positioning for the I, G, and Tab keys**
- **Employ preset tabs and word wrap**
- **Use 15-second timings to build keyboarding speed and accuracy**

## Getting Started

**Exercise 5.1** If you are continuing immediately from Session 4, you may skip the Exercise 5.1 warm-up drill. However, if you exited the Online Lab at the end of Session 4, warm up by completing Exercise 5.1. Refer to page 9 of Session 2 for instructions on logging on to the Online Lab and navigating to the appropriate exercise.

## Introducing the I, G, and Tab Keys

**Videos 5.1–5.3** The locations of the I, G, and Tab keys are shown in the following diagram. Watch Videos 5.1 through 5.3 and practice using these new keys.

**Exercises 5.2–5.9** Complete Exercises 5.2 through 5.8 to learn these new keys. Also complete the thinking drill, Exercise 5.9. When keying the drill lines, follow the instruction prompts in the Online Lab.

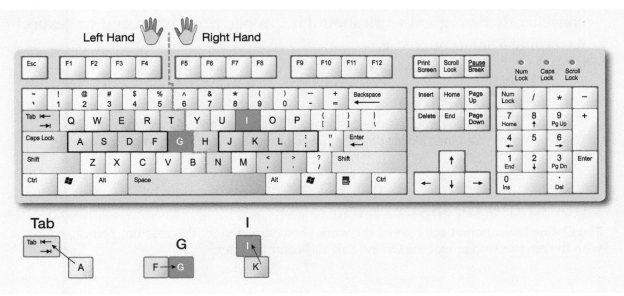

| Timings 27.2–27.3 | 1 | 2 | 3 | 4 | 5 |
|---|---|---|---|---|---|
| | 130 | 8 | 427 | 72 | 18724 |
| | 12.9 | 67.8 | 32.56 | 687.45 | 9.678 |
| | 14.87 | 67.21 | 978.12 | 4.872 | 96.78 |
| | 123.4 | 478.23 | 3.462 | 48.729 | 8.69 |
| | 1.456 | 2.789 | 34.620 | 72.94 | 687.89 |
| | 14.56 | 27.879 | 62.08 | 729.45 | 2 |
| | 56.21 | 87.90 | 620.81 | 25.2 | 672.3 |
| | 156.02 | 879.08 | 84.8 | 52.5 | 598 |
| | 47 | 56.49 | 61 | 98.12 | 390.26 |

For the following alphabetic timings, remember to press Tab at the start of the paragraph.

### 1-Minute Timings

**Timing 27.4**

The population of the United States has become more culturally varied. It is extremely important that individuals be made aware of the need to communicate with other cultures in ways that are satisfying to both parties. As people interact on a daily basis, meanings are discovered that form a bond for common understanding.

**Timing 27.5**

Basically, employers like a loyal employee. Honesty and courtesy always pay off in any job or assignment. Apathy and sloppy work are always very costly to a company. On the other hand, any employee who consistently does good work should be properly rewarded and can expect to receive a salary increase.

 **Ergonomic Tip**

To help you relax, occasionally lift your shoulders slowly while inhaling and then slowly drop them while exhaling. Repeat this exercise several times.

## Ending the Session

The Online Lab automatically saved the work you completed for this session. You can continue with the next session or exit the Online Lab and continue later.

## ➤➤ Reinforcing Your Skills

Complete Exercises 5.10 through 5.14 in the Online Lab. Reference the drill lines from the textbook as you key and keep your eyes on the textbook pages, not on your fingers. Complete each exercise at least once, but repeat exercises if you need more practice.

 **Success Tip**

Keeping your eyes on the source text helps your speed because if you look away, you will waste time finding your place again.

**Exercise 5.10**  I Drill

Key each line twice and push for speed.

1  if it in it it in kid kid his this fail fine file find
2  The kid thinks I had the idea that he did finish.

Key lines 3–5 once and then key the three lines again. Concentrate on control. Try to make fewer than two errors on each line.

3  Ill Inside Indeed If Illness Island Indeed Inside
4  She is a skilled athlete and likes little detail.
5  He did ski that hill. That is indeed a sad test.

**Exercise 5.11**  G Drill

Key each line twice and push for speed.

1  gal gal gas gas get get sag sag egg egg glee glee
2  Dennis and Gene nailed a slat in the fallen gate.

Key lines 3–5 once and then key the three lines again. Concentrate on control and try not to make errors.

3  Giant Giggle Glide Gentle Gene Gain Gift Glad Get
4  The endless agenda had eight legal details added.
5  Al tested his stiff leg. He gnashed his eight teeth.

| 6 | 7 | 8 | 9 |
|---|---|---|---|
| 66938 | 10.18 | 7.8 | 4.8 |
| 88282 | 7.85 | 67.8 | 21.6 |
| 775 | 8.94 | 67.21 | 41.72 |
| 993 | 15.63 | 478.231 | 687.452 |
| 5549 | 40.38 | 123.456 | 4.872 |
| 7970 | .89 | 1.456 | 48.729 |
| 2810 | 95.93 | 14.567 | 72.94 |
| 82 | 24.56 | 89.90 | 729.45 |
| 879 | 67.36 | .65 | 65.8 |
| 8322087 | 3.69 | | |

## Assessing Your Speed and Accuracy

Complete Timings 27.1 through 27.5 in the Online Lab. Refer to the following numerical timing text as you key.

Each timing will start as soon as you begin keying. If you finish keying before time expires, press Enter and start keying the timing text again.

The Online Lab specifies the WPM and error goals. When time expires, the Online Lab will give you a WPM rate and error report for the timing. The results of the timings will be stored in your Timings Performance report.

For the following numeric keypad timings that consist of columns of numbers, remember to press Enter after each number. Timings 27.2 and 27.3 use the same timing text.

### 1-Minute Timings

**Timing 27.1**

| 1 | 2 | 3 | 4 | 5 |
|---|---|---|---|---|
| 12 | 98 | 76 | 54 | 32 |
| 34 | 76 | 89 | 12 | 54 |
| 56 | 54 | 32 | 12 | 78 |
| 78 | 32 | 12 | 34 | 56 |
| 90 | 10 | 01 | 28 | 58 |
| 123 | 321 | 789 | 897 | 978 |
| 456 | 654 | 564 | 546 | 645 |
| 789 | 897 | 987 | 978 | 789 |
| 987 | 978 | 654 | 123 | 101 |
| 654 | 456 | 545 | 466 | 654 |
| 321 | 123 | 231 | 132 | 213 |
| 4321 | 1234 | 2413 | 1432 | 2431 |

**Exercise 5.12** Reinforcement Drill

Key the following drill lines once. Press Enter after each line. Your WPM rate will appear after keying each line. Try to reach 25 WPM (or the goal set by your instructor). Repeat this exercise to improve your speed.

1 His skin is thin; he is ill; he feels faint; see, he is ill.

2 He thinks it is a fad. I dislike that snide kid.

3 The kitten is a little lifeless and is an infant.

4 She shall indeed need that inside aid as enlisted.

5 His knife slid inside as the ill thief listened.

6 As the sled glides, the infant giggles in delight.

7 She disliked it. The kitten tangled that tinsel.

8 Jake, the gentle giant, giggled at Gina, the elf.

9 As she dashed ahead in glee, Leslie sang a jingle.

10 If he skis at night, Dad needs a light flashlight.

**Exercise 5.13** Tab Drill

The first line of a paragraph is commonly indented 0.5 inch from the left. Microsoft Word and many word processing programs have a default or preset tab stop every 0.5 inch across the page.

In this exercise, you will practice the Tab key reach and will see how the preset tabs work. Practice keying the following five columns of names in the Online Lab. Key the first word in the first column (Len), and then press Tab. Key the first word in the second column (Edna) and then press Tab, key Dale and then press Tab, key Nina and then press Tab, and then key Danita. Press Enter to move to the next line. Repeat the process for the remaining lines.

| | | | | | | | | | |
|---|---|---|---|---|---|---|---|---|---|
| 1 | Len | → | Edna | → | Dale | → | Nina | → | Danita |
| 2 | Jen | → | Tina | → | Dane | → | Dean | → | Thane |
| 3 | Tad | → | Ed | → | Gina | → | Kade | → | Neal |

## Introducing Word Wrap

Word wrap is a feature whereby text is continued on a new line when one line is full. The next word is automatically moved, or "wrapped," to the next line. When you key paragraphs of text (for example, in a letter or report), you do not need to press Enter at the end of each line. Be sure to press Enter to end a paragraph, however, because word wrap is a default setting.

4  Return the 420 reams of 16 lb. paper now, please.

5  She is purchasing a Group 857 biometrics system.

6  I would like to use 9 shades and 16 gray scales.

7  Send me 13 of Item 4 and 7 of Item 9 immediately.

8  West Arn 20 lb. paper has 99 percent rag content.

9  I have: 360 folders, 75 pencils, and 99 punches.

 **Success Tip**

Your persistence with keeping your eyes on the source text—rather than on your fingers, the keyboard, or the screen—will pay off in terms of speed and accuracy.

**Exercise 27.11**  **Keypad Reinforcement Drill**

In this drill, you will enter data vertically down a column by pressing Enter after each number. Key the following nine columns using the numeric keypad. Press Enter after each number. Concentrate on control and remember to think of large numbers in smaller groups as you key them.

| 1 | 2 | 3 | 4 | 5 |
|---|---|---|---|---|
| 654 | 687 | 78 | 08 | 19105 |
| 54 | 577 | 81 | 080 | 05084 |
| 76 | 575 | 8687 | 797 | 88 |
| 56 | 876 | 782 | 580 | 384 |
| 46 | 754 | 8422 | 680 | 18 |
| 767 | 796 | 789 | 4986 | 682 |
| 46 | 697 | 987 | 7984 | 9764 |
| 654 | 757 | 432 | 47782 | 7976 |
| 6054 | 885 | 8282 | 78853 | 8828 |
| 567 | 855 | 6732 | 88795 | 55130 |
| 7655 | 644 | 321 | 85 | 56 |
| 6054 | 54 | 989 | | |
| 456 | 66 | | | |

*drill continues*

**Exercise
5.14**   Word Wrap Drill

Key the two following paragraphs in the Online Lab. Press Tab to indent the first line of each paragraph and let word wrap move text to the next line automatically. Press Enter at the end of each paragraph.

1   →   An idle lad finishes last. He is shiftless as he sits and tells his tales. He needs an insight in the elegant things in life. An idle lad finishes last. He is shiftless as he sits and tells his tales.

2   →   Allan is attaining a skill in legal defense. The giant task is thankless. He insists that all the details heighten his thinking. Allan is attaining a skill in legal defense.

 **Ergonomic Tip**

Periodically rest your eyes by focusing for a short time on an object 20 or more feet away.

## Ending the Session

The Online Lab automatically saved the work you completed for this session. You can continue with the next session or exit the Online Lab and continue later. If you need to review the procedures for continuing to the next session or exiting the Online Lab, refer back to Session 1, page 8.

## Session 27 · Skills Reinforcement and Proficiency Exercises: Sessions 1–26

### Session Objectives

- **Review and practice correct finger positioning for the keys introduced in Sessions 1–26**
- **Utilize drills to practice keying**
- **Assess and reinforce keyboarding speed and accuracy with timings**

---

### Getting Started

**Exercise 27.1**  If you are continuing immediately from Session 26, you may skip the Exercise 27.1 warm-up drill. However, if you exited the Online Lab at the end of Session 26, warm up by completing Exercise 27.1.

### ⚞ Reinforcing Your Skills

**Exercises 27.2–27.8**  The exercises in this session are designed to reinforce your keyboarding skills of the alphabetic, number row, and numeric keypad keys. Begin this session work by completing Exercises 27.2 through 27.8 in the Online Lab. When keying the drill lines, follow the instruction prompts in the Online Lab. Complete each exercise at least once, but repeat exercises if you want to improve your WPM rate and accuracy.

Next, complete Exercises 27.9 through 27.11 in the Online Lab. For these exercises, reference the drill lines from the textbook as you key and keep your eyes on the textbook pages, not on your fingers. Complete each exercise at least once, but repeat exercises if you want to improve your WPM rate and accuracy.

**Exercise 27.9**  Sentences Drill

Key lines 1–3 once and push for speed. Key lines 1–3 again and concentrate on control.

1 It seems that I missed the road; it makes me angry.

2 Those wrecked cars were in the ditch at the curve.

3 Endure the thousand, routine, unexpected problems.

**Exercise 27.10**  Number Row Drill

Key lines 1–9 once and push for speed. Key lines 1–9 again and concentrate on control.

1 Find 5,000 medium-weight, legal-size file folders.

2 The Merkel 9000 offers 23 channels with 0.6 watts.

3 Please trace orders 1169, 2978, 67890, and 14989.

*drill continues*

## Session 6

# Skills Reinforcement and Proficiency Exercises: Sessions 1–5, Error Correction

### ⚑ Session Objectives

- Review and practice correct finger positioning for the keys introduced in Sessions 1–5
- Achieve the words per minute (WPM) and accuracy goals identified in the Online Lab
- Complete 10-second, 15-second, 20-second, and 1-minute timings
- Use timings to assess and reinforce keying speed and accuracy
- Differentiate between the Backspace and Delete keys
- Learn how to correct errors with the Backspace and Delete keys

## Getting Started

**Exercises 6.1–6.2** The first two exercises in this session are more than just warm-up drills. Exercise 6.1 is a speed timing drill and Exercise 6.2 is an accuracy timing drill. Complete these exercises even if you are continuing directly from Session 5.

The purpose of this session is to reinforce the keyboarding skills you have developed in the previous sessions. The timings in this session will help you to determine where you are in your skill development. The exercises in the session provide you with the opportunity to further work on improving your speed and accuracy.

This session also includes an introduction to the Backspace and Delete keys.

## Assessing Your Speed and Accuracy

Complete Timings 6.1 and 6.2 in the Online Lab using the paragraph at the top of the next page. In the Online Lab, you will start with a practice screen which you can use to practice keying the timing text without the timer running. When you have completed your practice, prompt the Online Lab to begin Timing 6.1. Both timings use the same paragraph. Once you are on an active timing screen, the timing will start as soon as you begin keying.

Remember to press Tab at the start of the paragraph. Do not press Enter at the end of each line, but only at the end of the paragraph. If you finish keying the paragraph before the timing expires, press Enter and start keying the paragraph again.

The Online Lab specifies WPM and error goals. When time expires, the Online Lab will give you a WPM rate and highlight any errors you made.

**Timings 26.2–26.3**

| 1 | 2 | 3 | 4 | 5 |
|---|---|---|---|---|
| 4.844 | 3748 | 568 | 345 | 34 |
| 6.673 | 3833 | 936 | 636 | 35 |
| 8.733 | 9374 | 947 | 663 | 36 |
| 5.663 | 0585 | 373 | 663 | 73 |
| 5.543 | 0392 | 464 | 663 | 93 |
| 3.323 | 0458 | 585 | 336 | 83 |
| 6.788 | 0382 | 484 | 393 | 23 |
| 6.733 | 0483 | 737 | 393 | 13 |
| 2.343 | 3230 | 363 | 993 | 30 |
| 2.3343 | 30339 | 922 | 993 | 54 |
| | | 291 | 339 | 65 |
| | | 302 | 936 | 63 |

For the following alphabetic timings, remember to press Tab at the start of the paragraph.

## 1-Minute Timings

**Timing 26.4**

 Students in school today must be prepared to live and compete in a global economy. They must develop a respect for life and work in a society of diverse cultures. Being exposed to the cultures of other countries can open doors to future job opportunities.

**Timing 26.5**

 The vessel sank in 510 feet of water in Lake Superior during a raging storm. An adept team of divers salvaged 149,683 parts. Seven local residents were among those who assisted in this job. The additional divers were welcome. The salvage company made a profit on their investment.

### Ergonomic Tip

Using a laptop or other mobile device to work remotely—outdoors or in a restaurant, for example—has its benefits, but different light sources can cause eye strain. Adjust your monitor's position to eliminate glare from light sources.

## Ending the Session

The Online Lab automatically saved the work you completed for this session. You can continue with the next session or exit the Online Lab and continue later.

### 1-Minute Timings

**Timings 6.1–6.2**

That gallant knight led the detail. A tall, thin lad assisted at the flank. The knight failed the task and feels the defeat. A sadness sifts in as his shield falls.

## Viewing the Timings Performance Report

The Online Lab provides a report showing the results of all of the document activities completed in the Online Lab. To view your Timings Performance report, complete the following steps:

1 Click the Course Menu button to open the Course Menu page.

2 Click *Reports* in the navigation pane.

3 Click *Timings Performance* to open the report. The report displays the results of all paragraph timings you have attempted. If you have attempted a timing more than once, the attempt with the highest WPM rate is shown.

4 Click *Attempts* to view results for all attempts and the text you keyed with errors marked.

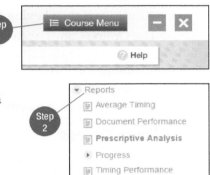

## Reinforcing Your Skills

The following speed and accuracy drills provide additional practice on the keys you have learned in Sessions 1–5. If you successfully keyed Timings 6.1 and 6.2, without hesitating, and met or exceeded the WPM and error goals specified in the Online Lab, proceed to the video introduction of the Backspace and Delete keys and the corresponding exercises in the Online Lab. However, if your WPM and error rates do not meet these goals, the speed and accuracy drills in this section will give you the opportunity for further practice.

If you have not mastered a key reach (you hesitate before striking the key) or if you are not keying at or above the Online Lab's WPM goals, key the speed drills, Exercises 6.3 and 6.4. If you are making more errors than specified in the Online Lab, key the accuracy drills, Exercises 6.5 and 6.6.

## Speed Drills

For the speed drills, key each line once as quickly as you can. After practicing the speed drills, either continue by completing the accuracy drills or go directly to Timing 6.3 to see if your speed has improved.

## Success Tip

The more you purposefully practice, the better your keyboarding skills should become.

## Assessing Your Speed and Accuracy

Complete Timings 26.1 through 26.5 in the Online Lab. Refer to the following numerical timing text as you key.

Each timing will start as soon as you begin keying. If you finish keying before time expires, press Enter and start keying the timing text again.

The Online Lab specifies the WPM and error goals. When time expires, the Online Lab will give you a WPM rate and error report for the timing. The results of the timings will be stored in your Timings Performance report.

For the following numeric keypad timings that employ columns of numbers, remember to press Enter after each number. Timings 26.2 and 26.3 use the same timing text.

### 1-Minute Timings

| Timing 26.1 | 1 | 2 | 3 | 4 | 5 |
|---|---|---|---|---|---|
| | 34 | 345 | 568 | 37.48 | 4844 |
| | 35 | 636 | 936 | 38.33 | 6673 |
| | 36 | 663 | 947 | 93.74 | 8733 |
| | 73 | 663 | 373 | 05.85 | 5663 |
| | 93 | 663 | 464 | 03.92 | 5543 |
| | 83 | 336 | 585 | 04.58 | 3323 |
| | 23 | 393 | 484 | 03.82 | 6788 |
| | 13 | 393 | 737 | 04.83 | 6733 |
| | 30 | 993 | 363 | 32.30 | 2343 |
| | 54 | 93 | 922 | 30.339 | 23343 |
| | 65 | 339 | 291 | | |
| | 63 | 936 | 302 | | |

**Exercise 6.3**  Balanced-Hand Words Drill

Balanced-hand words contain letters that require switching back and forth from your left to right hand to key the letters. Key each line once. Focus on speed.

1  and the ant sit ale elf end hen she end sigh sign
2  aid fit sit did tie die dig fig and the hang then
3  halt than hand lens lake lane then than sign fish

4  idle lens lane sigh then dish disk sign half lake
5  shake snake title aisle angle fight handle island
6  angle sight digit gland eight slant height sleigh
7  signal giant tight an he if it and elf the and he

**Exercise 6.4**  Letter Combinations Drill

The following combinations focus on common letter sequences found in many words. Key each line once. Focus on speed.

1  de den dead deal desk denial dense deft dental
2  di dig dish dial digest dislike dine dike disk
3  I dislike the heat dial that fits the dental fan.

4  fi fish final fine finish fight find fig field finale
5  ga gal gas gag gale gait gallant gasket gadget
6  Gale finished the gasket at the gas gadget gate.

7  ha hate halt half hash hang hand handle hat had
8  ki kite kindle kilt kiln king kink kit kind
9  That hanging kite tail has halted the hail.

10  le lest left lead lend ledge least leaf lean lease
11  li lid lie lied line link linking linkage like
12  At least link the left lid and let the length stand.

13  sa sad sat safe sake sale said sang Sal saline
14  si sit site sitting signal sighted sill silken siding
15  Sad Sal sang a signal as she sighted a safe site.

16  st stead steal steadiness stateside stag state
17  ta tag talk take tale taste task tan tall tail
18  Steadfast Stella stands and talks and then sits.

*drill continues*

## Exercise 26.11 Keypad Reinforcement Drill

Key columns 1–9 once. Concentrate on keying with control so your results will be as accurate as possible. Remember to press Enter after each number.

| 1 | 2 | 3 | 4 | 5 |
|---|---|---|---|---|
| .41 | 100 | 4111 | 24 | 456 |
| .41 | 104 | 1444 | 56 | 789 |
| .51 | 145 | 4568 | 25 | 125 |
| .61 | 414 | 1787 | 58 | 125 |
| .71 | 151 | 1679 | 47 | 128 |
| .81 | 149 | 88981 | 71 | 124 |
| .91 | 109 | 98871 | 89 | 126 |
| .11 | 011 | 019091 | 80 | 129 |
| 1.41 | 084 | 001001 | 20 | 125 |
| 1.41 | 171 | | 20 | 128 |
| 1.41 | 155 | | 20 | 982 |
| 1.41 | 109 | | 50 | 982 |
| 1.45 | 18 | | 50 | 12 |
| 1.46 | | | 20 | |
| 1.4 | | | 70 | |
| | | | 45 | |
| | | | 86 | |

| 6 | 7 | 8 | 9 |
|---|---|---|---|
| 2222 | 345 | 5.68 | 4844 |
| 2525 | 636 | 9.36 | 6673 |
| 2582 | 663 | 9.47 | 8733 |
| 2582 | 663 | 3.73 | 5663 |
| 9792 | 663 | 4.64 | 5543 |
| 2728 | 336 | 5.85 | 3323 |
| 26267 | 393 | 4.84 | 6788 |
| 88771 | 393 | 7.37 | 6733 |
| 07862 | 993 | 3.63 | 2343 |
| 72 | 993 | 9.22 | 23343 |
| | 339 | 2.91 | 2657 |
| | 936 | 3.02 | |
| | 93 | 3.0 | |

19 te tea test tenth tend tenant tease teak tent

20 th then that than thing this theft thin thesis

21 Then that tested tenant, Ted, did a tenth test.

## Accuracy Drills

For the following accuracy drills, key each group of lines once. Concentrate on control as you key. After practicing the accuracy drills, go directly to Timing 6.3 to see if your accuracy has improved.

 **Success Tip**

Concentrate on keying with control for accuracy as you type the lines in the accuracy drills. Remember that your mind controls your fingers!

**Exercise 6.5** Double-Letter Words Drill

These words require you to key the same letter twice in a row. Your finger does not need to return to the home row between identical letters. Key each line once. Focus on control.

1 see glee needs indeed feeling needless teens seed

2 egg sell sniff haggle falling eggshell stall eggs

3 eel keen sheen needle fiddles seedling sleek deed

4 add kiss stiff assist endless lifeless still hill

5 fee need sheet seeing dissent likeness steed heel

6 add fell skill allied skilled settling shell tell

7 see feel teeth indeed gallant sledding sleet knee

8 all hall shall little install knitting stall tall

9 Sadness is a feeling I assess as an alleged need.

10 Assist the skiing attendant and lessen all falls.

11 The sleek kitten shall flee the illegal attendants.

12 Haggling is a senseless dissent that is needless.

13 Flatten the stiff fiddle and install the tassels.

**Exercise 26.10**  Keypad 3 Drill

Key columns 1–5 once and push for speed. Key columns 1–5 again and concentrate on accuracy. Remember to press Enter after each number.

| 1 | 2 | 3 | 4 | 5 |
|---|---|---|---|---|
| 63 | 36 | 45.6 | 464 | 2343 |
| 63 | 73 | 38.3 | 585 | 2334 |
| 63 | 73 | 83.8 | 484 | 4873 |
| 63 | 93 | 93.8 | 737 | 4848 |
| 63 | 83 | 73.6 | 363 | 3929 |
| 36 | 23 | 37.3 | 922 | 26282 |
| 36 | 13 | 36.9 | 291 | 4844 |
| 36 | 30 | 93.6 | 302 | 6673 |
| 36 | 54 | 96.3 | 30 | 8733 |
| 36 | 65 | 3.3 | 4435 | 5663 |
| 93 | 63 | 56.8 | 4344 | 55 |
| 39 | 36 | 93.6 | 3345 | |
| 39 | 83 | 94.7 | 3443 | |
| 39 | 49 | 37.3 | | |
| 69 | 34 | | | |
| 69 | 234 | | | |
| 63 | 354 | | | |
| 34 | 345 | | | |
| 35 | | | | |

**Exercise 6.6** Longer Words Drill

Longer words require more concentration, which leads to better accuracy. Keep your eyes on the copy as you key. Key each line once. Focus on control.

1 endless athlete flatten inflated install disliked
2 lenient distant delighted heading inkling digital
3 A lenient athlete has inflated the flattened keg.

4 hesitating likeness indefinite alkaline initiated
5 heightened stealing gaslight lengthened delegates
6 The hesitating delegate is stealing the gaslight.

7 landslide skinflint stateside essential legislate
8 negligent lightness sightless delighted attendant
9 tasteless steadfast defendant thankless seashells
10 Seashells in the landslide delighted a skinflint.

## Assessing Your Speed and Accuracy

Now that you have practiced the appropriate speed and accuracy drills, complete two 1-minute timings using the following paragraph. (This is the same text keyed for Timings 6.1 and 6.2.)

Each timing will begin as soon as you begin keying. Remember to press Tab at the start of the paragraph. If you finish keying the paragraph before the timing expires, press Enter and start keying the paragraph again.

When time expires, the Online Lab will give you a WPM rate and will show you any errors you made in the keyed text. The results of all of your timings will be stored in your Timings Performance report. (If you need to review the procedure for viewing your Timings Performance report, refer back to page 24.) Compare your rates from Timings 6.3 and 6.4 to your rates from Timings 6.1 and 6.2. Has your speed improved? Do you have fewer errors? If you are not reaching the Online Lab's WPM and error goals, repeat Sessions 1–5.

### 1-Minute Timings

**Timings 6.3–6.4**

That gallant knight led the detail. A tall, thin lad assisted at the flank. The knight failed the task and feels the defeat. A sadness sifts in as his shield falls.

Keypad 2 Drill

Key columns 1–5 once and push for speed. Key columns 1–5 again and concentrate on accuracy. Remember to press Enter after each number.

| 1 | 2 | 3 | 4 | 5 |
|---|---|---|---|---|
| 52 | 25 | 242 | 222 | 24.56 |
| 52 | 62 | 252 | 224 | 27.89 |
| 52 | 72 | 252 | 225 | 20.10 |
| 52 | 82 | 262 | 226 | 24.56 |
| 52 | 92 | 852 | 227 | 26.78 |
| 52 | 02 | 258 | 228 | 25.25 |
| 25 | 42 | 158 | 228 | 245.67 |
| 25 | 52 | 148 | 822 | 278.90 |
| 25 | 27 | 284 | 922 | 124.56 |
| 25 | 85 | 282 | 202 | 1.27 |
| 25 | 58 | 272 | 202 | |
| 24 | 85 | 958 | 212 | |
| 24 | 95 | 594 | 2169 | |
| 42 | 96 | | | |
| 62 | 90 | | | |
| 72 | 88 | | | |
| 82 | 56 | | | |
| 52 | 24 | | | |

# Introducing the Backspace and Delete Keys

**Videos 6.1–6.2** The locations of the Backspace and Delete keys are shown in the following diagram. Watch Videos 6.1 and 6.2 and practice the reaches for these new keys.

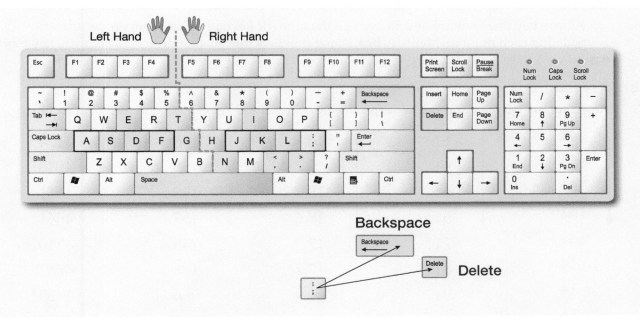

The Backspace and the Delete keys are both used to correct text. However, they produce corrections in different ways.

Pressing the Backspace key will delete the character to the left of the insertion point. In other words, the Backspace key deletes backward from the insertion point. The Backspace key is a good choice to use if you immediately realize you have pressed the wrong character key when keying text.

Pressing the Delete key will delete the character to the right of the insertion point. In other words, pressing the Delete key deletes forward from the insertion point. To make a correction in text using the Delete key, use the arrow keys or mouse to position the insertion point immediately before the character to be deleted, press the Delete key to remove the incorrect character, and then press the correct character key.

Complete Exercises 6.7 and 6.8 in the Online Lab but follow the step instructions shown in the textbook.

**Exercise 6.7** Backspace Drill

To practice correcting with the Backspace key, complete the following steps in Exercise 6.7 in the Online Lab. The steps will direct you to key intentional errors and then will direct you to fix them using the Backspace key.

1  Key the following:

> The hesitatint

2  Press the Backspace key to delete the letter *t* in the keyed line. The text should read *The hesitatin*.

3  Press the G key so the text reads *The hesitating*.

*drill continues*

##  Reinforcing Your Skills

Complete Exercises 26.8 through 26.11 in the Online Lab. Refer to the following columns of drill line numbers as you key and keep your eyes on the textbook pages, not on your fingers. Complete each exercise at least once, but repeat exercises if you want to improve your WPM rate or accuracy.

As you key these columnar drill lines on the numeric keypad, press Enter on the numeric keypad after each number. Mentally break long numbers into smaller groups to help you key more easily.

**Exercise 26.8**

### Keypad 1 Drill

Key columns 1–5 once and push for speed. Key columns 1–5 again and concentrate on accuracy.

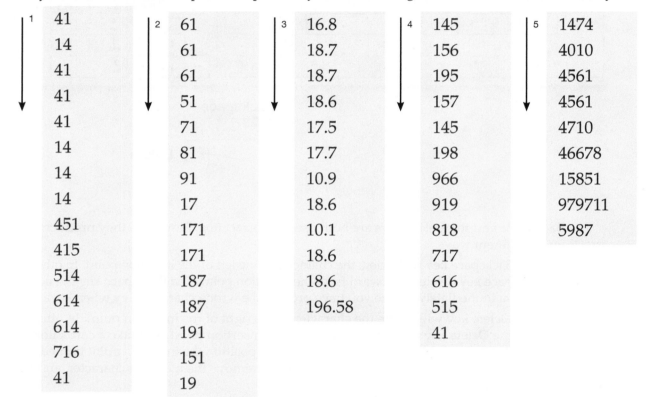

| 1 | 2 | 3 | 4 | 5 |
|---|---|---|---|---|
| 41 | 61 | 16.8 | 145 | 1474 |
| 14 | 61 | 18.7 | 156 | 4010 |
| 41 | 61 | 18.7 | 195 | 4561 |
| 41 | 51 | 18.6 | 157 | 4561 |
| 41 | 71 | 17.5 | 145 | 4710 |
| 14 | 81 | 17.7 | 198 | 46678 |
| 14 | 91 | 10.9 | 966 | 15851 |
| 14 | 17 | 18.6 | 919 | 979711 |
| 451 | 171 | 10.1 | 818 | 5987 |
| 415 | 171 | 18.6 | 717 | |
| 514 | 187 | 18.6 | 616 | |
| 614 | 187 | 196.58 | 515 | |
| 614 | 191 | | 41 | |
| 716 | 151 | | | |
| 41 | 19 | | | |

**4** Press the spacebar and then key the following:

> delegate is te

**5** Press the Backspace key twice to delete *te*. The text should read *The hesitating delegate is*.

**6** Key the following:

> stealing the gas l

**7** Press the Backspace key twice to delete *l* and the space after *gas*.

**8** Key the following:

> light.

**9** Proof your final line to make sure it reads *The hesitating delegate is stealing the gaslight*.

**Exercise 6.8** Delete Drill

To practice correcting with the Delete key, complete the following steps in Exercise 6.8 in the Online Lab. The steps will direct you to key intentional errors and then will direct you to fix them by positioning the insertion point using the arrow keys or the mouse and the Delete key.

**1** Key the following:

> That tenant, Ted, did the alleged deed.

**2** Position the insertion point immediately to the left of the *T* in *Ted*.

**3** Press the Delete key three times, once for each character in the name *Ted*. This action will delete the name from the sentence.

**4** Key the following:

> Dale

**5** Proof the text to confirm that it reads *That tenant, Dale, did the alleged deed*.

**6** Position the insertion point immediately to the left of the *a* in *That*.

**7** Press the Delete key twice to delete the letters *a* and *t*.

**8** Key the following:

> e

**9** Proof the text to confirm that it reads *The tenant, Dale, did the alleged deed*.

 **Ergonomic Tip**

If your mouse is separate from your keyboard, keep the mouse at the same height and distance from you as the keyboard.

## Ending the Session

The Online Lab automatically saved the work you completed for this session. You can continue with the next session or exit the Online Lab and continue later. You can also review the results of the timings completed in the Online Lab by reviewing your Timings Performance report.

# Session 26

## 1, 2, 3

### Session Objectives

- **Identify the 1, 2, and 3 keys on the numeric keypad**
- **Practice correct finger positioning for the numeric keypad's 4, 1, 2, and 3 keys**
- **Learn to key numbers in columns**

## Getting Started

**Exercise 26.1** If you are continuing immediately from Session 25, you may skip the Exercise 26.1 warm-up drill. However, if you exited the Online Lab at the end of Session 25, warm up by completing Exercise 26.1.

## Introducing the 1, 2, and 3 Keys on the Numeric Keypad

**Videos 26.1–26.3** The location of the 1, 2, and 3 keys on the numeric keypad are shown in the following diagram, and the reaches are demonstrated in Videos 26.1 through 26.3.

**Exercises 26.2–26.7** Complete Exercises 26.2 through 26.4 to learn these new keys. Exercises 26.5 through 26.7 provide practice keying using the alphabetic keys. When keying the drill lines, follow the instruction prompts in the Online Lab.

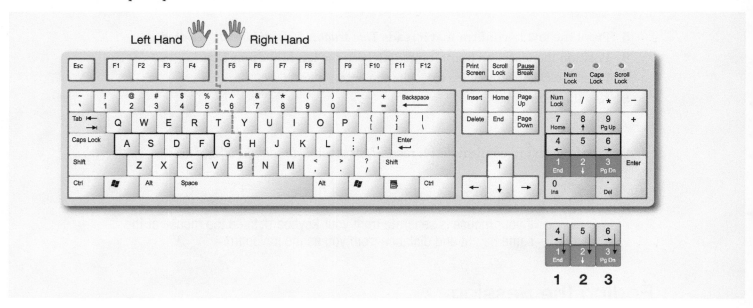

## Session 7 — P, R, Question Mark

# P, R, Question Mark

## Session Objectives

- **Identify the P, R, and question mark (?) keys**
- **Practice correct finger positioning for the P, R, and question mark keys**
- **Complete 15-second and 1-minute timings to improve keyboarding speed and accuracy**
- **Explore common keyboarding errors**

## Getting Started

**Exercise 7.1**  If you are continuing immediately from Session 6, you may skip the Exercise 7.1 warm-up drill. However, if you exited the Online Lab at the end of Session 6, warm up by completing Exercise 7.1.

## Introducing the P, R, and Question Mark Keys

**Videos 7.1–7.3**  The locations of the P, R, and question mark (?) keys are shown in the following diagram. Watch Videos 7.1 through 7.3 and practice using these new keys.

**Exercises 7.2–7.7**  Complete Exercises 7.2 through 7.6 to learn these new keys. Also complete the thinking drill, Exercise 7.7. When keying the drill lines, follow the instruction prompts in the Online Lab.

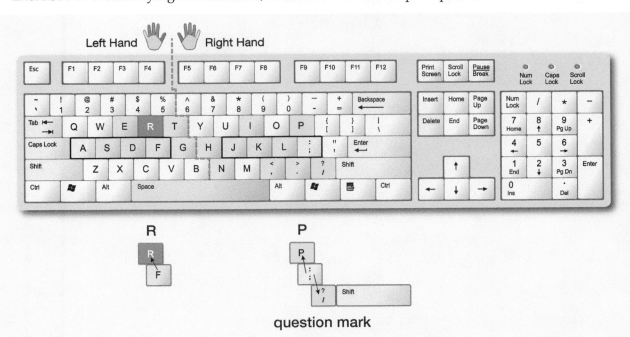

question mark

For the following alphabetic timings, remember to press Tab at the start of the paragraph.

1-Minute Timings

**Timing 25.4**

   Traveling in this vast land is a great experience. The endless rivers, vast prairies that stretch as far as the eye can see, and mountains that reach for the sky are all impressive. Rural villages reveal something of the past in terms of how they are laid out. These vivid scenes revive the mind and lift the spirits.

**Timing 25.5**

   During your working life, you will meet and work with people of many different cultures. Although each of us is a member of a racial or ethnic group, our work groups make up one large community. The beliefs we share give us a common base and a list of topics to discuss.

 **Ergonomic Tip**

To relax your fingers, lightly clench your hand and then release, fanning out fingers. Repeat five times.

## Ending the Session

The Online Lab automatically saved the work you completed for this session. You can continue with the next session or exit the Online Lab and continue later.

## 🦅 Reinforcing Your Skills

Complete Exercises 7.8 through 7.11 in the Online Lab. Reference the drill lines from the textbook as you key and keep your eyes on the textbook pages, not on your fingers. Complete each exercise at least once, but repeat exercises if you need more practice.

**Exercise 7.8**  P Drill

Key each line twice and push for speed. Try to reach 25 WPM (or the goal set by your instructor). Your WPM rate will appear after keying each line.

1  ;p pan pat pea peg pen pep pet pie pig pin pit pails
2  ;p ship tape pink skip slap taps gaps pest sap paste
3  Peasant Pennant Pitfall Patient Pheasant Pleasant Philadelphia

Key lines 4–6 once and then key the three lines again. Concentrate on control. Try to reach 25 WPM and make two or fewer errors (or follow the goals set by your instructor). Your WPM rate will appear after keying each line, and any errors will be highlighted.

4  A tall, split, peeling aspen sapling is diseased.
5  Pat speaks and pleads and defends the plaintiffs.
6  Did Jane tape that splint and dispense the pills?

**Exercise 7.9**  R Drill

Key each line twice. Push for speed the first time you key a line and concentrate on control the second time. Try to reach 25 WPM (or the goal set by your instructor). Your WPM rate will appear after keying each line.

1  fr rain rare real rink rake rage rear ripe rip rage rigid
2  stare there their after pride tired far her press jar tear
3  Refrain Repress Release Retreat Resident Register Reap

**Exercise 7.10**  Question Mark Drill

Press the spacebar only once after the question mark (?) at the end of a sentence. This rule applies to all end-of-sentence punctuation. When a question mark ends a line in the drill, press Enter immediately. Do not press the spacebar first.

Key lines 1–3 and then key the lines again. Concentrate on control. Try to reach 25 WPM (or the goal set by your instructor). Your WPM rate will appear after keying each line.

1  Is Jennie ahead? Is Dennis safe? Is Allen late?
2  Is Ken late? Is Dale fit? Is Neil in his teens?
3  Did she dine? Did the leaf fall? Did Jena flee?

**Exercise 25.11** — Keypad 9 Drill

Key rows 1–4 once and push for speed. Key rows 1–4 again and concentrate on accuracy.

| | | | | | | | | | |
|---|---|---|---|---|---|---|---|---|---|
| 1 | 66 | 69 | 69 | 99 | 96 | 96 | 66 | 90 | 90 |
| 2 | 90 | 98 | 97 | 797 | 894 | 869 | 759 | 6599 | 9589 |
| 3 | 695 | 696 | 697 | 698 | 699 | 789 | 798 | 788 | 799 |
| 4 | 6979 | 69879 | 69879 | 69857 | 96857 | 9678 | 9687 | 898 | 999 |

**Exercise 25.12** — Keypad Reinforcement Drill

Key the following rows once. Concentrate on keying as accurately as possible.

| | | | | | | | | | | | | |
|---|---|---|---|---|---|---|---|---|---|---|---|---|
| 1 | 876 | 568 | 678 | 468 | 780 | 786 | 807 | 876 | 558 | 558 | 778 | 788 |
| 2 | 45678 | 87654 | 80765 | 876 | 8888 | 7787 | 7877 | 6778 | 5678 | 458 | 775 | 499 |
| 3 | 900 | 909 | 969 | 969 | 696 | 898 | 797 | 690 | 578 | 589 | 987 | 95 |
| 4 | 96.78 | 96.87 | 89.85 | 96.78 | 967.45 | 456.78 | 567.89 | 987.65 | 976.54 | 4.56 | 6.65 | 6.5 |
| 5 | 05058 | 60060 | 54904 | 85358 | 79964 | 84946 | 89757 | 48965 | 80086 | 478 | 489 | 450 |

## Assessing Your Speed and Accuracy

Complete Timings 25.1 through 25.5 in the Online Lab. Refer to the following numerical timing text as you key.

Each timing will start as soon as you begin keying. If you finish keying before time expires, press Enter and start keying the timing text again.

The Online Lab specifies the WPM and error goals. When time expires, the Online Lab will give you a WPM rate and error report for the timing. The results of the timings will be stored in your Timings Performance report.

For the following numeric keypad timings, remember to press Tab between number groups and Enter at the end of each row. Timings 25.2 and 25.3 use the same timing text.

**1-Minute Timings**

**Timing 25.1**

| | | | | | | | | | | | |
|---|---|---|---|---|---|---|---|---|---|---|---|
| 99 | 89 | 89 | 79 | 79 | 66 | 69 | 69 | 59 | 59 | 49 | 49 |
| 789 | 789 | 456 | 456 | 475 | 678 | 789 | 908 | 970 | 970 | 987 | 09 |
| 900 | 909 | 909 | 969 | 696 | 898 | 797 | 690 | 578 | 589 | 987 | 95 |
| 9678 | 9687 | 8985 | 6978 | 96745 | 45678 | 56789 | 98765 | 98765 | 7584 | 7605 | 4557 |
| 9889 | 8899 | 9999 | 7999 | 69969 | 69969 | 94569 | 49566 | 59469 | 8940 | 4875 | 4658 |

**Timings 25.2–25.3**

| | | | | | | | | | | | |
|---|---|---|---|---|---|---|---|---|---|---|---|
| 9889 | 8899 | 9999 | 7999 | 69969 | 69969 | 94569 | 49566 | 59469 | 7059 | 6587 | 6789 |
| 900 | 909 | 909 | 969 | 969 | 696 | 898 | 797 | 690 | 578 | 589 | 987 |
| 9678 | 9687 | 8985 | 6978 | 96745 | 45678 | 56789 | 98765 | 98765 | 9876 | 446 | 5579 |
| 789 | 789 | 456 | 456 | 475 | 678 | 789 | 908 | 970 | 970 | 987 | 09 |
| .99 | .89 | .89 | .79 | .79 | .66 | .69 | .69 | .59 | .59 | .49 | .49 |

**Exercise**  **Reinforcement Drill**

**7.11** Key lines 1–3 once and push for speed. Try to reach 25 WPM (or the goal set by your instructor). Your WPM rate will appear after keying each line.

1 In the sleet, a sheep passed the pines and plants.

2 In his pastel sedan, Jake passed that fast jeep.

3 His left thigh is gashed; the patient is in pain.

 **Success Tip**

Think control as you key each line. If you make more than two errors on a line, repeat it. Keep your eyes on the copy in the text as you key.

Key lines 4–9 once. Concentrate on control. Try to reach 25 WPM and make two or fewer errors (or follow the goals set by your instructor). Your WPM rate will appear after keying each line, and any errors will be highlighted.

4 rest tree trip hire ring fire earn hard dirt fair

5 range ridge raise reign rinse art jar rinse right

6 eager fir ran after heart large dress greed green

7 Shall I still slide in the infield if Jake faints?

8 Has she hit? Has the thief left? Has he landed?

9 Is Dale fit? Is Neil in his teens? Is Ken late?

## Identifying Common Keyboarding Errors

Some errors affect only the appearance of a document. On the other hand, certain keyboarding errors can have a drastic effect on the message being communicated. Consider the result of transposing (switching) two numbers in a customer's invoice, such as keying $19 instead of $91. Following is a list of some common keyboarding mistakes. Reviewing this list will help you be aware of possible errors as you complete timings and later as you prepare letters and other documents.

- Keying wrong words
- Transposing numbers or letters
- Placing extra spaces between words or numbers
- Placing a space before a punctuation mark
- Not capitalizing a proper noun or the first word of a sentence
- Capitalizing a word in a sentence that should not be capitalized
- Placing too many spaces after a punctuation mark or between paragraphs
- Using improper left, right, top, or bottom margins
- Not indenting properly
- Being inconsistent in vertical spacing
- Using incorrect punctuation

## ➤➤ Reinforcing Your Skills

Complete Exercises 25.8 through 25.12 in the Online Lab. Reference the drill lines from the textbook as you key and keep your eyes on the textbook pages, not on your fingers. Complete each exercise at least once, but repeat exercises if you want to improve your WPM rate or accuracy.

As you key these drill lines on the numeric keypad, press Tab on the alphabetic keyboard between numbers and press Enter on the numeric keypad at the end of each row. Mentally break long numbers into smaller groups to help you key more easily.

**Exercise 25.8**  Keypad 7 Drill

Key rows 1–4 once and push for speed. Key rows 1–4 again and concentrate on accuracy.

| | | | | | | | | | | | |
|---|---|---|---|---|---|---|---|---|---|---|---|
| 1 44 | 47 | 47 | 47 | 55 | 57 | 57 | 57 | 66 | 67 | 67 | 67 |
| 2 76 | 74 | 74 | 567 | 567 | 765 | 765 | 4567 | 4567 | 7 | 456 | 457 |
| 3 65 | 45 | 67 | 4567 | 6 | 777 | 765 | 7567 | 5560 | 57670 | 5666 | 056 |
| 4 70 | 45670 | 45670 | 567 | 5560 | 5456 | 6747 | 44760 | 547 | 645 | 747 | 757 |

**Exercise 25.9**  Keypad Decimal Point Drill

Key rows 1–4 once and push for speed. Key rows 1–4 again and concentrate on accuracy.

| | | | | | | |
|---|---|---|---|---|---|---|
| 1 45.7 | 74.5 | 56.5 | 65.4 | 67.4 | 74.7 | 75.0 |
| 2 5.00 | 6.75 | 6.50 | 7.50 | 7.45 | 5.50 | 6.50 |
| 3 1.5 | 5.1 | 6.47 | 7.50 | 5.5 | 4.4 | 7.6 |
| 4 .75 | .50 | 4.00 | 6.75 | 56.70 | 7.75 | .755 |

**Exercise 25.10**  Keypad 8 Drill

Key rows 1–4 once and push for speed. Key rows 1–4 again and concentrate on accuracy.

| | | | | | | |
|---|---|---|---|---|---|---|
| 1 888 | 585 | 588 | 855 | 858 | 787 | 568 |
| 2 850 | 857 | 758 | 457 | 458 | 758 | 848 |
| 3 800 | 888 | 886 | 855 | 758 | 846 | 468 |
| 4 007 | 780 | 786 | 807 | 876 | 558 | 855 |

 **Success Tip**

Keep your wrist straight and above the keyboard while using the numeric keypad.

## Assessing Your Speed and Accuracy

Complete Timings 7.1 and 7.2 in the Online Lab to assess the skills you have learned in this session. Refer to the following paragraphs as you key.

Each timing will start as soon as you begin keying. Remember to press Tab at the beginning of all paragraphs in timings. If you finish keying a paragraph before the timing expires, press Enter and start keying the paragraph again.

If you are not reaching your WPM goals on your drills, push for speed when you key these timings. If you are keying at or above your WPM goals but are not meeting your error goals, concentrate on accuracy. When time expires, the Online Lab will give you a WPM rate and will show you any errors you made. The results will be stored in your Timings Performance report.

### 1-Minute Timings

**Timing 7.1**
Jena prepares legal papers and letters. She prefers reading ledgers and graphs. It is tiring and drains her. If she falters at the start, Jena is risking a defeat. The stern leader sees her stress and praises her spirit.

**Timing 7.2**
Print the paragraph in large letters. Raise the title and delete the digraphs. Insert three fresh phrases at the end. It is all right if Dane deletes that first phrase. It is a danger and a threat. Perhaps the ending is right.

### Ergonomic Tip

Never rest the palm of your hands or wrists on the keyboard, wrist rest, or table while typing. Wrist rests are useful when taking breaks from typing.

## Ending the Session

The Online Lab automatically saved the work you completed for this session. You can continue with the next session or exit the Online Lab and continue later.

# Session

# 25

# 7, 8, 9, Decimal Point

## Session Objectives

- Identifty the 7, 8, 9, and decimal point (.) keys on the numeric keypad
- Practice correct finger positioning for the numeric keypad's 7, 8, 9, and decimal point (.) keys
- Practice keying numbers in rows

## Getting Started

**Exercise 25.1** If you are continuing immediately from Session 24, you may skip the Exercise 25.1 warm-up drill. However, if you exited the Online Lab at the end of Session 24, warm up by completing Exercise 25.1.

## Introducing the 7, 8, 9, and Decimal Point Keys on the Numeric Keypad

**Videos 25.1–25.4** The location of the 7, 8, 9, and decimal point (.) keys on the numeric keypad are shown in the following diagram, and the reaches are demonstrated in Videos 25.1 through 25.4.

**Exercises 25.2–25.7** Complete Exercises 25.2 through 25.5 to learn these new keys. Exercises 25.6 and 25.7 provide practice keying using the alphabetic keys. When keying the drill lines, follow the instruction prompts in the Online Lab.

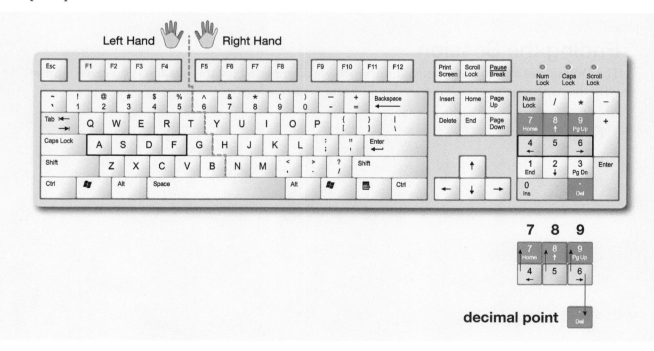

## Session
## 8
# M, O

## Session Objectives

- **Identify the M and O keys**
- **Practice correct finger positioning for the M and O keys**
- **Improve keyboarding speed and accuracy with timings**
- **Spell words correctly when keyboarding**

## Getting Started

**Exercise 8.1** If you are continuing immediately from Session 7, you may skip the Exercise 8.1 warm-up drill. However, if you exited the Online Lab at the end of Session 7, warm up by completing Exercise 8.1.

## Introducing the M and O Keys

**Videos 8.1–8.2** The locations of the M and O keys are shown in the following diagram. Watch Videos 8.1 and 8.2 and practice using these new keys.

**Exercises 8.2–8.8** Complete Exercises 8.2 through 8.7 to learn these new keys. Also complete the thinking drill, Exercise 8.8. When keying the drill lines, follow the instruction prompts in the Online Lab.

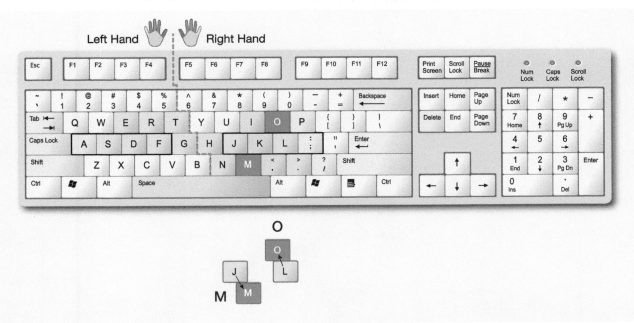

For the following alphabetic timings, remember to press Tab at the start of the paragraph.

1-Minute Timings

**Timing 24.4**

The way you shut down your computer is important because the proper procedure avoids losing unsaved data and properly saves systems settings. Use features with names such as Sleep or Hibernate to save computer power but still be able to return to your desktop and any running programs quickly without having to reboot.

**Timing 24.5**

Spreadsheet software is an electronic version of the ruled worksheets accountants used in the past. Spreadsheet software provides a means of organizing, calculating, and presenting financial, statistical, and other numerical information. For example, an instructor may use a spreadsheet to calculate student grades.

 Ergonomic Tip

Keep your neck and shoulders relaxed as you key.

## Ending the Session

The Online Lab automatically saved the work you completed for this session. You can continue with the next session or exit the Online Lab and continue later.

## Reinforcing Your Skills

Complete Exercises 8.9 through 8.11 in the Online Lab. Reference the drill lines from the textbook as you key and keep your eyes on the textbook pages, not on your fingers. Complete each exercise at least once, but repeat exercises if you want to improve your WPM rate or accuracy.

**Exercise 8.9** M Drill

Key each drill line twice and push for speed. Try to reach 25 WPM (or the goal set by your instructor). Your WPM rate will appear after keying each line.

1 jm am am him him man man mad mad jam jam me me mean

2 might might metal metal dream dream ram ram made made

3 Mashed Mean Mailed Minted Melted Makes Melt Might Mild

Key lines 4–6 once and then key the three lines again. Concentrate on control. Try to reach 25 WPM and make two or fewer errors (or follow the goals set by your instructor). Your WPM rate will appear after keying each line, and any errors will be highlighted.

4 Mike is making a frame; he needs ample sandpaper.

5 Did Mamie transmit the message after amending it?

6 Did Sammie eliminate all mistakes in the message?

**Exercise 8.10** O Drill

Key each drill line twice and push for speed. Try to reach 25 WPM (or the goal set by your instructor). Your WPM rate will appear after keying each line.

1 lo do go no to of on or doe off one too mom dot not for ton

2 roof look room toot noon foot food soon moon doom root

3 Order Older Folder Online Option Model Morning Oasis Operate

Key lines 4–6 once and then key the three lines again. Concentrate on control. Try to reach 25 WPM and make two or fewer errors (or follow the goals set by your instructor). Your WPM rate will appear at the end of each line, and any errors will be highlighted.

4 Does Norman Olson look for those options noted on the form?

5 The golf pro told the people to look for good golf partners.

6 The donations for the top ten projects are right on target.

**Exercise 24.8** Keypad Reinforcement Drill

Key rows 1–9 once. Concentrate on keying as accurately as possible. Press Tab between numbers. Press Enter after each row.

| | | | | | | | | | | | | |
|---|---|---|---|---|---|---|---|---|---|---|---|---|
| 1 | 654 | 654 | 456 | 456 | 456 | 456 | 456 | 655 | 556 | 556 | 664 | 664 | 56 |
| 2 | 456 | 546 | 546 | 546 | 645 | 456 | 546 | 566 | 566 | 664 | 665 | 444 | 44 |
| 3 | 544 | 544 | 566 | 544 | 644 | 644 | 554 | 555 | 444 | 655 | 444 | 555 | 44 |
| 4 | 64 | 456 | 456 | 654 | 456 | 666 | 444 | 555 | 654 | 654 | 456 | 456 | 456 |
| 5 | 45 | 666 | 555 | 444 | 654 | 654 | 465 | 55 | 44 | 45 | 65 | 64 | 56 |
| 6 | 500 | 600 | 400 | 545 | 545 | 6545 | 4505 | 5460 | 5440 | 5540 | 50404 | 54 | 446 |
| 7 | 644 | 654 | 4560 | 4560 | 4560 | 4560 | 6540 | 6540 | 6540 | 450 | 406 | 654 | 604 |
| 8 | 556 | 654 | 6540 | 5460 | 5046 | 0564 | 0546 | 5040 | 5000 | 605 | 404 | 4055 | 64 |
| 9 | 600 | 500 | 4000 | 4005 | 5004 | 6005 | 5004 | 6005 | 0665 | 044 | 606 | 505 | 606 |

## Assessing Your Speed and Accuracy

Complete Timings 24.1 through 24.5 in the Online Lab. Refer to the following numerical timing text as you key.

Each timing will start as soon as you begin keying. If you finish keying before time expires, press Enter and start keying the timing text again.

The Online Lab specifies the WPM and error goals. When time expires, the Online Lab will give you a WPM rate and error report for the timing. The results of the timings will be stored in your Timings Performance report.

For the following numeric keypad timings, remember to press Tab between numbers (not digits) and Enter at the end of each row. Timings 24.2 and 24.3 use the same timing text.

### 1-Minute Timings

**Timing 24.1**

| | | | | | | | | | | | | |
|---|---|---|---|---|---|---|---|---|---|---|---|---|
| 654 | 654 | 654 | 456 | 456 | 666 | 444 | 555 | 546 | 546 | 546 | 456 | 46 |
| 555 | 666 | 444 | 555 | 654 | 555 | 456 | 456 | 654 | 645 | 645 | 645 | 45 |
| 654 | 654 | 456 | 456 | 456 | 456 | 456 | 655 | 556 | 556 | 664 | 664 | 56 |
| 456 | 546 | 546 | 546 | 645 | 456 | 546 | 566 | 566 | 644 | 665 | 444 | 44 |
| 544 | 544 | 566 | 544 | 644 | 644 | 554 | 555 | 444 | 655 | 444 | 555 | 44 |

**Timings 24.2–24.3**

| | | | | | | | | | | |
|---|---|---|---|---|---|---|---|---|---|---|
| 550 | 600 | 540 | 540 | 650 | 6540 | 6440 | 4560 | 6540 | 6054 | 56605 |
| 500 | 600 | 400 | 545 | 545 | 6545 | 4505 | 5460 | 5440 | 5540 | 50404 |
| 644 | 654 | 4560 | 4560 | 4560 | 4560 | 6540 | 6540 | 6540 | 450 | 406 |
| 556 | 654 | 6540 | 5460 | 5046 | 0564 | 0546 | 5040 | 5000 | 605 | 404 |
| 600 | 500 | 4000 | 4005 | 5004 | 6005 | 5004 | 6005 | 0665 | 044 | 606 |

## Exercise 8.11   Reinforcement Drill

Key the following drill lines once. Press Enter after each line. Try to reach 25 WPM and make two or fewer errors (or follow the goals set by your instructor). Your WPM rate will appear after keying each line, and any errors will be highlighted.

1. The malt that Pam made had milk and mint in it.
2. The fine farm animal, Sandman, had a marked limp.
3. Mail the letter at midnight and add ample stamps.

4. Is that smashed metal mass a damaged helmet, Jim?
5. As her mind dimmed, Minnie missed the main message.
6. In April, Tonia Jones took her first plane ride to a remote island.

7. She told those on the longest list to find roommates for ten months.
8. Look for people that are doing the right things for the team.
9. The Golden Age is something to look for in their lifelong plans.
10. Look for the person that likes to do things that are not right.

## Assessing Your Speed and Accuracy

Complete Timings 8.1 through 8.6 in the Online Lab to assess the skills you have learned in this session. Refer to the following paragraphs as you key.

Each timing will start as soon as you begin keying. Remember to press Tab at the start of the paragraph. If you finish keying the paragraph before the timing expires, press Enter and start keying the paragraph again.

The Online Lab specifies WPM and error goals. When time expires, the Online Lab will give you a WPM rate and will show you any errors you made. The results will be stored in your Timings Performance report.

### 1-Minute Timings

**Timing 8.1**
Marna smelled the simmering meat. The steam permeated the air. She managed a small taste and smiled. The meat and milk might help that little girl and ease her pain.

**Timing 8.2**
As he firmed the damp earth at the tree, the miser imagined he heard a small sigh. Mirages in the misted marsh alarmed him. Grim fears emerged as his mindless tramping faltered.

**Timing 8.3**
Make that simple diagram first and then send a message in the mail. Tell that salesman that his latest remarks made the manager mad. The meeting impaired the imminent merger.

As you key these drill lines on the numeric keypad, press Tab between number groups and press Enter when you reach the end of each row. The Tab key is located to the left of the alphabetic keys, and the Enter key is on the numeric keypad. Mentally break long numbers into smaller groups to help you key more easily. Review the instructions in Session 14 on breaking down large numbers into smaller groups, if needed.

**Exercise 24.6** Keypad Home Row Drill

Key rows 1–5 once and push for speed. Key rows 1–5 again and concentrate on accuracy. Place your right hand on home row (4, 5, 6). Tab between numbers (for example, after the digit "6" in the first number, "456"). Press Enter after each row.

| | | | | | | | | | | | | | |
|---|---|---|---|---|---|---|---|---|---|---|---|---|---|
| 1 | 456 | 456 | 456 | 654 | 654 | 654 | 546 | 546 | 546 | 564 | 564 | 645 | 65 |
| 2 | 444 | 445 | 455 | 454 | 555 | 564 | 565 | 566 | 645 | 654 | 644 | 554 | 46 |
| 3 | 555 | 556 | 554 | 445 | 446 | 444 | 666 | 654 | 655 | 645 | 564 | 546 | 54 |
| 4 | 666 | 655 | 654 | 645 | 555 | 546 | 564 | 566 | 544 | 546 | 466 | 455 | 64 |
| 5 | 464 | 465 | 646 | 454 | 455 | 556 | 564 | 565 | 566 | 654 | 666 | 546 | 55 |

**Exercise 24.7** Keypad 0 Drill

Key rows 1–5 once and push for speed. Key rows 1–5 again and concentrate on accuracy. Use your right thumb for the 0 key. Press Tab between numbers. Press Enter after each row.

| | | | | | | | | | | | |
|---|---|---|---|---|---|---|---|---|---|---|---|
| 1 | 0 | 00 | 000 | 000 | 000 | 000 | 50 | 50 | 50 | 50 | 50 |
| 2 | 400 | 400 | 400 | 500 | 500 | 500 | 500 | 600 | 600 | 500 | 400 |
| 3 | 405 | 504 | 506 | 605 | 440 | 400 | 550 | 660 | 660 | 550 | 440 |
| 4 | 440 | 500 | 450 | 450 | 560 | 4560 | 4560 | 4650 | 6540 | 6540 | 56000 |
| 5 | 550 | 600 | 540 | 540 | 650 | 6540 | 6440 | 4560 | 6405 | 6054 | 56005 |

 **Success Tip**

Building your skill with the numeric keypad will allow you to enter numerical data quickly and accurately.

**Timing 8.4**

More and more people are looking for homes that are near shopping areas, homes with ample parking spots, and good mortgage rates. Realtors are eager to help people find their dream homes.

**Timing 8.5**

Those people that are doing things to help others represent feelings that are not forgotten. The time spent doing things for others is one of the easier things to do that makes one feel good. It is important to help others.

**Timing 8.6**

Those people who fish together are often times looking for other lakes to get the fish that dreams are made of. These people tell great stories from their past fishing trips. Their trophies are important to them.

 **Ergonomic Tip**

To help prevent shoulder and neck pain while typing, make sure your shoulders are relaxed, your upper arms are rested at your side, and your forearms are roughly parallel to the floor. You may need to adjust the height of your office chair to find a comfortable position.

## Ending the Session

The Online Lab automatically saved the work you completed for this session. You can continue with the next session or exit the Online Lab and continue later.

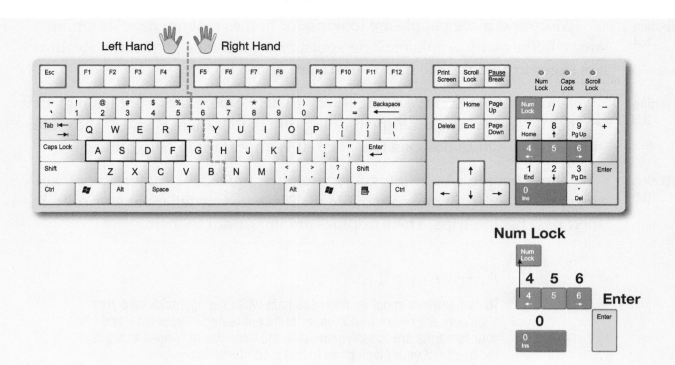

**Videos
24.1–24.4**

Video 24.1 presents the hand position for the home row keys on the numeric keypad, Video 24.2 provides reinforcement on the use of the Tab key to the left of the alphabetic keys. Video 24.3 presents the 0 key reach on the numeric keypad. Finally, Video 24.4 presents the Num Lock key reach.

**Exercises
24.2–24.5**

Complete Exercises 24.2 and 24.3 to learn these new keys. Exercises 24.4 and 24.5 provide practice keying using the alphabetic keys. When keying the drill lines, follow the instruction prompts in the Online Lab.

## Alternate Numeric Keypad Configurations

Many laptop computers do not have a separate numeric keypad. Instead, they have an embedded numeric keypad, which includes the symbol keys +, –, /, and *. The embedded numeric keyboard can be activated when the function key is used with some of the right-hand alphabetic keys.

To use an embedded numeric keyboard on a laptop computer, look for Num Lock on a function key. Use the appropriate command to turn Num Lock on or off—probably holding down the function key (FN or Fn, near the spacebar) while tapping the appropriate function key on the top row. When Num Lock is on, place your JKL; (semicolon) fingers on the keys designated for 4, 5, 6 (likely the UIO keys) as the numeric keypad home row. You can now use the alphabetic keyboard as a numeric keyboard.

When keying numeric text, use the semicolon (;) finger to reach the Enter key.

## 🐾 Reinforcing Your Skills

Complete Exercises 24.6 through 24.8 in the Online Lab. Reference the drill lines from the textbook as you key and keep your eyes on the textbook pages, not on your fingers. Complete each exercise at least once, but repeat exercises if you want to improve your WPM rate or accuracy.

## Session

# 9

## U, B, W

### Session Objectives

- **Identify the U, B, and W keys**
- **Practice correct finger positioning for the U, B, and W keys**
- **Apply critical thinking quickly while keyboarding**

### Getting Started

**Exercise 9.1** If you are continuing immediately from Session 8, you may skip the Exercise 9.1 warm-up drill. However, if you exited the Online Lab at the end of Session 8, warm up by completing Exercise 9.1.

### Introducing the U, B, and W Keys

**Videos 9.1–9.3** The locations of the U, B, and W keys are shown in the following diagram. Watch Videos 9.1 through 9.3 and practice using these new keys.

**Exercises 9.2–9.10** Complete Exercises 9.2 through 9.9 to learn these new keys. Also complete the thinking drill, Exercise 9.10. When keying the drill lines, follow the instruction prompts in the Online Lab.

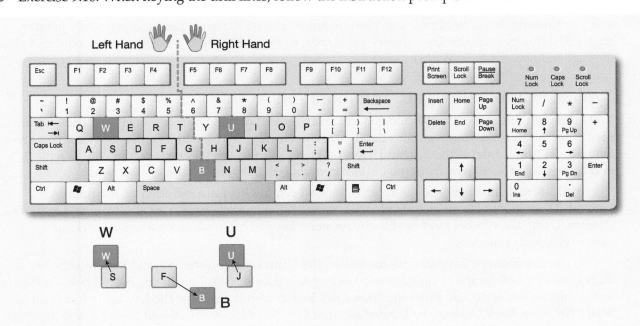

# Session
# 24

# 4, 5, 6, 0, Enter, Num Lock

## Session Objectives

- **Explore the typical numeric keypad configuration and the Num Lock key**
- **Identify the numeric keypad's home row (4, 5, 6), 0, and Enter keys**
- **Practice correct finger positioning for the numeric keypad's 4, 5, 6, 0, and Enter keys**
- **Learn to key numbers in rows**

## Getting Started

**Exercise 24.1** If you are continuing immediately from Session 23, you may skip the Exercise 24.1 warm-up drill. However, if you exited the Online Lab at the end of Session 23, warm up by completing Exercise 24.1.

## Introducing the Numeric Keypad

Computer keyboards typically have a numeric keypad, sometimes referred to as the *number pad*, located to the right of the alphabetic keys. The numeric keypad allows you to enter numeric data with one hand. You can use this keypad instead of the numeric row above the alphabetic keys. A common use of the numeric keypad includes entering numbers in cells and rows of spreadsheets. With a minimum amount of practice, you can enter numeric data at speeds significantly greater than 100 digits per minute. By industry standards, a rate of 250 digits per minute is considered average (equivalent to 50 WPM).

### Typical Numeric Keypad Configuration

The following illustration shows the general arrangement of most numeric keypads. The bottom row of the numeric keypad contains the 0 (zero), decimal point (.), and Enter keys. The second row from the bottom contains the 1, 2, and 3 keys. The third row is the home row and contains the 4, 5, and 6 keys. The fourth row from the bottom contains the 7, 8, and 9 keys.

In addition to the numbers 0 through 9, several symbol keys are included on the numeric keypad. These symbol keys include plus (+), minus (–), diagonal or forward slash (/), and asterisk (*) keys. Using the symbol keys next to the numeric keypad often saves time when working extensively with numbers.

To use the numeric keypad on a computer, the Num Lock (Numeric Lock) key must be on. A light usually displays above the numeric keypad to indicate Num Lock is on. Num Lock is a toggle key. If Num Lock is not on, press the *Num Lock* key to turn it on. Press the key again to turn it off. *Note: The Num Lock key may be labeled as Num Loc, Num Lk, or NL. When Num Lock is disabled, alternate functions that control the insertion point are active on several numeric keypad keys.*

When working with spreadsheets or tables, use the Tab key (keyed with the A finger) to move across the screen from cell to cell. Use the Enter key (located to the right of the 3 and decimal point keys on the numeric keypad) to move vertically down a column from one row to the next.

## ✎ Reinforcing Your Skills

Complete Exercises 9.11 through 9.14 in the Online Lab. Reference the drill lines from the textbook as you key and keep your eyes on the textbook pages, not on your fingers. Complete each exercise at least once, but repeat exercises if you need more practice.

**Exercise 9.11**    U Drill

Key each line twice and push for speed. Try to reach 25 WPM (or the goal set by your instructor). Your WPM rate will appear after keying each line.

1  ju put put sun sun fun fun mud mud gum gum sum sum

2  under audit rumor truth about nurse sprung refund blunt

3  Fusion Lawful Nature Urgent Plural Module Suppose

Key lines 4–6 once and then key the three lines again. Concentrate on control. Try to reach 25 WPM and make two or fewer errors (or follow the goals set by your instructor). Your WPM rate will appear after keying each line, and any errors will be highlighted.

4  Just be sure to return that blouse to the bureau.

5  That auto bumper is a hunk of junk; it is ruined.

6  A stout runner shouted and slumped to the ground.

**Exercise 9.12**    B Drill

Key each line twice and push for speed. Try to reach 25 WPM (or the goal set by your instructor). Your WPM rate will appear after keying each line.

1  fb bad bag ban bar bat bed beg Ben bet bid big bit

2  barter member harbor banker ballot border benefit brake

3  Alphabet Basement Neighbor Remember Remarkable Be

Key lines 4–6 once and then key the three lines again. Concentrate on control. Try to reach 25 WPM and make two or fewer errors (or follow the goals set by your instructor). Your WPM rate will appear after keying each line, and any errors will be highlighted.

4  I grabbed a dab of bread and biked to the harbor.

5  Babe is baffled; the bulkiest bottles are broken.

6  Barni, the beagle, barks and begs for a big bone.

**Exercise 9.13**    W Drill

Key each line twice and push for speed. Try to reach 25 WPM (or the goal set by your instructor). Your WPM rate will appear after keying each line.

1  sw jaw wag raw two war wet saw hew how new sew snow

2  rewind warmer bowler wiring inward wisdom gawkers

3  Hardware Workable Weakness Endowment Two Window

*drill continues*

# Unit 4

# Numeric Keypad Keys

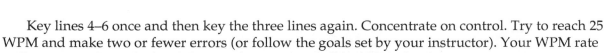

Key lines 4–6 once and then key the three lines again. Concentrate on control. Try to reach 25 WPM and make two or fewer errors (or follow the goals set by your instructor). Your WPM rate will appear at the end of each line, and any errors will be highlighted.

4 Wear a warm gown if it snows; the weather is raw.

5 The new lawn will grow when watered well at dawn.

6 It is wise to wire the news to the waiting woman.

**Exercise 9.14**  Reinforcement Drill

Key lines 1 and 2 once for speed. Try to reach 25 WPM (or the goal set by your instructor). Your WPM rate will appear after keying each line.

1 ju put put sun sun fun fun mud mud gum gum sum sum

2 haunt audit rumor truth about nurse sprung refund blunt

Key line 3 once. Concentrate on control. Try to reach 25 WPM (or the goal set by your instructor). Your WPM rate will appear after keying the line.

3 Fusion Lawful Nature Urgent Plural Module Suppose

Follow the previous procedures and key lines 4 and 5 once for speed. Key line 6 once for speed, while also concentrating on control.

4 Beneath the bridge in the brook, the bears bathed.

5 He is bitter and bleak; the dark banjo is broken.

6 A nimble rabbit blinks and nibbles bean blossoms.

Follow the previous procedures and key lines 7 and 8 once for speed. Key line 9 once for speed, while also concentrating on control.

7 Will Marlow wash in warm water that wool sweater?

8 With a white towel, Warren wiped the jeweled bowl.

9 If Win washes the new window, is he wasting water?

**Exercise 9.15**  Thinking Drill

Using the following initial letters, key as many words as you can think of that begin with the letters given:

bu    bi    wo    wh

Key the words in a list. Key all the "bu" words first, and then go to the next set of letters. Try to think of at least 10 words. If you can think of 20 to 30 words, that's great. Insert a space after each word and press Enter between the different word sets.

**Ergonomic Tip**

Use your entire hand to get to hard-to-reach keys rather than forcing your hands into awkward positions. Make sure you bring your fingers back to the home row keys.

## Ending the Session

The Online Lab automatically saved the work you completed for this session. You can continue with the next session or exit the Online Lab and continue later.

## Assessing Your Speed and Accuracy

Complete Timings 9.1 through 9.6 in the Online Lab to assess the skills you have learned in this session. Refer to the following paragraphs as you key.

Each timing will start as soon as you begin keying. Remember to press Tab at the start of the paragraph. If you finish keying the paragraph before the timing expires, press Enter and start keying the paragraph again.

The Online Lab specifies WPM and error goals. When time expires, the Online Lab will give you a WPM rate and will show you any errors you made. The results will be stored in your Timings Performance report.

### 1-Minute Timings

**Timing 9.1**

The blunt auditor suggested to Duke that the business returns were a huge fraud. The usual routine of minimum adjusting of funds had been sound, but a fortune of thousands paid to a juror had not been inserted in the annual input. Duke presumed he was ruined and flushed with guilt.

**Timing 9.2**

Ruth sulked as her aunt poured a dose of the awful blue fluid. The sour stuff was supposed to be used for fatigue from the flu. She paused for a minute and gulped it down. Her aunt found four lumps of sugar as a bonus. Sullen disgust would turn into a laugh as a result.

**Timing 9.3**

Biff booked a berth on the battered boat. As he bragged to his somber brother, the boom of the harbor bells trembled. Beneath the boasting, Biff began to babble. A belated bolt of disbelief and brooding stabbed at him.

**Timing 9.4**

Labor to do a noble job. Bosses like brains and ambition. A blend of both brings a desirable habit that boosts a beginner. A babbling boaster absorbs a bore. The absent laborer blemishes his possible bankroll boost.

**Timing 9.5**

We will await the word of warning in the new tower. The wise, stalwart leader wants to worship the writings of men of worth. He frowns on wrong, narrow swine. We will follow wise wishes and win a wearisome war and bestow a renewed foothold.

**Timing 9.6**

Will rehashed the written words. He did not wish to show that witless newsman how shallow his words were. However, he wanted to warn the world of the wasted wealth in the wages of the man. He showed the network the handwriting on the wall.

1-Minute Timings

**Timing 23.1**

Barlow, a shrewd fellow, winked as he waited in the shadows. A whistle warned him of the slow walk of his fellow worker. As he wallowed in the warmth of that workshop, Will worked in the wild, blowing wind. Barlow was worthless.

**Timing 23.2**

Malaysia is in the process of shifting from an agricultural to an industrial economy. Their government has a plan entitled Vision 2020 that will make them fully industrialized by that year. Many government and business people feel that the ethnic balance of Malay, Chinese, and Indian races must remain intact. Banks are offering low-interest loans for Malay-owned businesses.

**Timing 23.3**

A lazy bicycle ride in the country is surely a healthy and worthy activity. A sunny sky and a dry day is surely an omen to any type of cyclist. Be wary of cloudy and windy days. A daily remedy for a healthy and spry body is a ride on a cycle. Both the young and not so young enjoy biking.

3-Minute Timings

**Timings 23.4–23.5**

The Transportation Security Authority (TSA) has announced it will be trial testing a new prescreening program that could offer some airline passengers expedited screening through US security checkpoints. Travel Fast Airlines is pleased to announce our partnership with the TSA in testing this new concept at our hubs in Dallas/Fort Worth and Miami. You may be eligible to participate and potentially be cleared through the TSA pre-vetting process, resulting in some screening benefits at the checkpoint. During the first phase of testing, certain frequent flyers who are US citizens, as well as members of Customs and Border Protection's Global Entry, NEXUS, and SENTRI programs, will be eligible to participate in this pilot program which could qualify them for expedited screening. The TSA will determine who participates in the trial on a per-flight segment basis.

**Ergonomic Tip**

Experiment with your screen colors to find the combination that is most comfortable for you. Avoid using light-colored characters on the screen. Instead, use dark characters on a light-colored background.

## Ending the Session

The Online Lab automatically saved the work you completed for this session. You can continue with the next session or exit the Online Lab and continue later.

7  Take #33 and move it to #66. Move #66 to #1234.

8  Farber & Daughters is the name of my law firm.

9  The check was made out for at least $*,***,***.99.

10  You scored 89% on the exam and 78% on the drill.

11  Now is the time (11:45) for you (Ginny) to move.

12  I make $9 per hour, but I would like to make $16.

13  Sixteen @ $1.23 and 57 @ $23.45 is far too much.

14  If hours = 40 and rate = $5.00, then gross = $200.

15  The equation was A = B + C + F + D + G + H + I + J.

16  Jerry thought that A < B and F < G and JK < JKL.

17  However, Tom knew that A > B and F > G and I > IK.

18  If you raise 2^2, the answer will be squared now.

19  Enter your last name on the line that follows: _____.

20  LET X = A + B + C / D * H * (HH - K) + (HH + JJ).

21  Go to http://ppi-edu.com for information on course availability.

22  IF GH < AN AND TH > HJ OR TY < TU, MOVE TRY TO A.

23  There will be a reaction--perhaps not good--if you do that.

24  PRINT TAB[17] "PLAYER" TAB[34] "FG PERCENT"; FG

25  The #12 category weighs 18#; the #7 category weighs 6#.

 **Success Tip**

> If you hesitated while keying or are unsure of the reaches required
> for symbols in Exercise 23.15, repeat the appropriate exercises in the
> sessions in Unit 3.

## Assessing Your Speed and Accuracy

Complete Timings 23.1 through 23.5 in the Online Lab. Refer to the following paragraphs as you key. Timings 23.4 and 23.5 use the same paragraph of text.

Each timing will start as soon as you begin keying. Remember to press Tab at the start of the paragraph. If you finish keying the paragraph before the timing expires, press Enter and start keying the paragraph again.

The Online Lab specifies the WPM and error goals. When the time expires, the Online Lab will give you a WPM rate and error report for the timing. The results of the timings will be stored in your Timings Performance report.

# Session 10

# Skills Reinforcement and Proficiency Exercises: Sessions 1–9

## ▶▶▶ Session Objectives

- **Review and practice correct finger positioning for the Sessions 1–9 keys**
- **Employ successful keyboarding skills to build speed and accuracy**

---

**Exercise 10.1**

## Getting Started

If you are continuing immediately from Session 9, you may skip the warm-up drill at the start of this session. However, if you exited the Online Lab at the end of Session 9, warm up by completing Exercise 10.1.

The purpose of this session is to reinforce the keyboarding skills you have developed in the previous sessions. The timings in this session will help you to determine where you are in your skill development, and the exercises in the session provide you with the opportunity to further work on improving your skill and accuracy.

## Assessing Your Speed and Accuracy

Complete Timings 10.1 and 10.2 in the Online Lab using the paragraph below. In the Online Lab, you will start with a practice screen that you can use to practice keying the timing text without the timer. Both timings use the same paragraph. Once you are on an active timing screen, the timing will start as soon as you begin keying.

Remember to press Tab at the beginning of the paragraph. Also, do not press Enter at the end of each line, but only at the end of the paragraph. If you finish keying the paragraph before the timing expires, press Enter and start keying the paragraph again.

The Online Lab specifies WPM and error goals. When time expires, the Online Lab will give you a WPM rate and will show you any errors you made. The results of both timings will be stored in your Timings Performance report.

### 1-Minute Timings

**Timings 10.1–10.2**

When the winter snow thaws, warm rain washes the world. Wild flowers begin to flutter in a slow swing with the wind. Whiffs of a meadow awakened swirl down at the dawn. The dew is a rainbow and twinkles as a jewel. Winter has blown onward.

**Exercise 23.12** Greater Than and Less Than Drill

As with the less than symbol (<), the greater than symbol (>) can be keyed with a space before and after it or with no space. Whichever you select, be consistent.

Key lines 1–3 once and then key the lines again. Concentrate on control. Anchor the J finger for this reach and use the left Shift key. *Note: The first drill line contains lowercase Ls and the third line contains number 1s.*

1  l<l l<l ;<; ;<; 6>4 6>2 5>1 9>7 l>l ;>>;;

2  L>M L>R ;>; 56 > 43 126 > 78 198 > 48 66 > 55 6>>

3  6 > 2 < 6; 6 > 1.2; 78 > 8; 1234 > 678; 56 < 234;

**Exercise 23.13** Diagonal Drill

The diagonal symbol (/) is used as a division sign in computer programming languages and in Web addresses such as http://www.emcp.com. It is also used to divide characters such as the month, day, and year in a date (for example, 04/14/97). The diagonal is sometimes called the *forward slash* or simply *slash*.

Key lines 1–3 once and then key the lines again. Concentrate on control. Anchor the J finger when making this reach.

1  ;/; ;/; ;/; /;/ ;/; ;/; /;/ ;/; /;/ ;/ ;/ ;/;/ ;/

2  a = b/c d = f/g h=j/l t=k/j r = j / k fgh = rty/j

3  The equation: miles/hours will equal speed rate.

**Exercise 23.14** Backslash Drill

Key lines 1–3 once and then key the lines again. Concentrate on control. Do not press the Shift key. Anchor the J finger when making this reach.

1  The \ sign is used to designate a given file path.

2  For example, c:\windows will take you to windows in C drive.

3  c:\user\pat\documents\guestlist c:\braymore\lrp\minutes

**Exercise 23.15** Reinforcement Drill

Key each line once. *Hint: The blank answer line in this drill should be keyed as a series of 10 underscores.*

1  Two-thirds of the three-fourths are very gifted.

2  John said: Data Structures is a great textbook.

3  Jerome's cat ran to Mary's house and said "meow"!

4  "Hello," said Jim. "How are you this fine day?"

5  "Help!" yelled the old man as the bees followed.

6  If the dress is $35.95, why is the coat $125.75?

*drill continues*

## ▶▶ Reinforcing Your Skills

The following speed and accuracy drills provide additional practice on the keys you have learned in Sessions 7–9. If you successfully keyed Timings 10.1 and 10.2 and met or exceeded the goals specified in the Online Lab, proceed to Session 11. However, if your WPM and error rates do not match these goals, the speed and accuracy drills in this section will give you the opportunity for further practice.

If you have not mastered a key reach (you hesitate before striking the key) or if you are not keying at or above the Online Lab's WPM goals, key the speed drills, Exercises 10.2 through 10.4. If you are committing more errors than the goal specified in the Online Lab, key the accuracy drills, Exercises 10.5 and 10.6.

### Speed Drills

For the speed drills, key each line once and try to make your fingers go faster as you key the lines. After practicing the speed drills, either continue by completing the accuracy drills or go directly to Timing 10.3 to see if your speed has improved.

**Exercise 10.2**  Keys Review Drill

Key each line once. Focus on speed.

1  asdf jkl; ;p; frf jmj fbf lol fbf sws pr mt db wm

2  p pad pan peg pen pin pit pie plan phase pledge plane

3  r rap ran red rip rent rests real repels refers roam rope

4  m ham hem men him mate mind mesh manage mandate

5  u up upper under urge utmost unit utter until untold umpire

6  o oh or odd old one oaf opens omit ogle order of oblong

7  b bad beg bid bop brag blend board brake better bowl

8  w was wed who win woe were when went where with

9  Shannon Olan Bronson George Janet Kent Martin John

**Exercise 10.3**  Balanced-Hand Words Drill

Key each line once. Focus on speed.

1  lamb blend bland blame amble emblem problem bible

2  lap nap pen paid pane flap span pale spent dispel

3  air pan sir risks lair heir pair hair flair widow

4  map maid mane melt sham lame mend firm make flame

5  due burn turn dug fuel tug rug Bud bug gut guru bus rub tub

6  fog sod oak rod foam fork form foam odor soak rod

*drill continues*

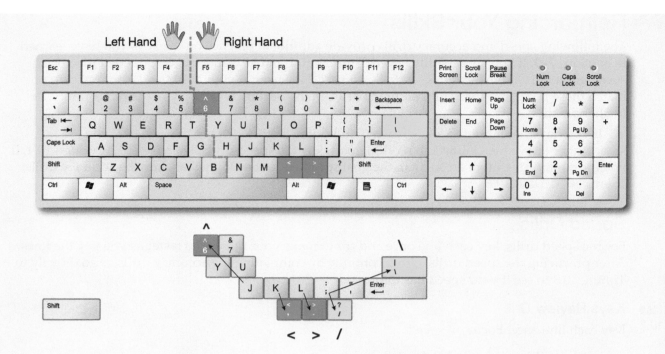

## ❯❯ Reinforcing Your Skills

Complete Exercises 23.10 through 23.15 in the Online Lab. Reference the drill lines from the textbook as you key and keep your eyes on the textbook pages, not on your fingers. Press Enter after each line. Complete each exercise at least once, but repeat exercises if you want to improve your WPM rate or accuracy.

**Exercise 23.10 Circumflex Accent Drill**

Key lines 1–3 once and then key the lines again. Concentrate on control. Anchor the semicolon (;) finger when making this reach and remember to press the left Shift key.

1 j6j j6j j6j j^j j^j j^j j^j J^J J^J J^J J^J J^J J^

2 The ^ sign is used to raise an integer to a power.

3 For example, 2^2 is the square of the numeral two.

**Exercise 23.11 Less Than Drill**

The less than symbol (<) can be keyed with a space before and after it or with no space. Whichever you select, be consistent. Anchor the J or the semicolon (;) finger when making this reach and remember to use the left Shift key.

Key lines 1–3 once and then key the lines again. Concentrate on control.

1 2<7 3<8 4<9 5<6 8<9 1<2 5<7 6<8 k<l k<l 5<6 1<8<9

2 12 < 43 16 < 58 17 < 89 15 < 28 123 < 456 17 < 77

3 2 < 4, j < k, 1 < m, K < L; S < Z; K < L; JK < LM

7 bow wig wow vow down gown wisp with wish when wit

8 Did the lame lamb amble down to the big, pale oak?

9 The pale widow paid for the vivid gown and a wig.

10 When did Bob mend the pair of problem emblems?

**Exercise 10.4** Two-Letter Combinations Drill
Key each line once. Focus on speed.

1 pe peg pen pest pets pert peso petite petition

2 pi pin pie piles pipes pink pine pig piston pilot

3 That petite person with pets had piles of pinkish pills.

4 ra ran rap ranks rake rates raised range rapid random

5 ri rid rip rises ripe right ridges rigid rinse rigs rim

6 Rapid Red ran to the raised ridges on that range.

7 ma man mat math make mail marsh manager margin

8 mi mid mild mind mint midst might misting mire mite

9 The manager might mail the mild mints to the man.

10 bu bud bus bun burn bust butter bullet build button builder

11 du due duke dust dull dud dues dumb dusk duo dunk dug

12 The bus tour took us to Utah to see multiple mountain ranges.

13 oa oak oats oath oatmeal load toad roast float oasis

14 The oath at the oak tree oasis was about oats.

15 ba bad bag bail balk bath badge barks bandages bald

16 bl blade bleak blast blank blight blind blinks blow

17 The bat blinked at a baboon blinded in bandages.

18 wa was war wag wade wait wane wash waste warm want

19 wi win wit wig wide wipe will wise wield wiper window

20 Winna washed and wiped her window; she wasted water.

## Session 23 | Circumflex Accent, Less Than, Greater Than, Diagonal, Backslash

### Session Objectives

- Identify the circumflex accent (^), less than symbol (<), greater than symbol (>), diagonal (/), and backslash (\) keys
- Practice correct finger positioning for the circumflex accent (^), less than symbol (<), greater than symbol (>), diagonal (/), and backslash (\) keys

---

### Getting Started

**Exercise 23.1** If you are continuing immediately from Session 22, you may skip the Exercise 23.1 warm-up drill. However, if you exited the Online Lab at the end of Session 22, warm up by completing Exercise 23.1.

### Introducing the Circumflex Accent, Less Than, Greater Than, Diagonal, and Backslash Symbol Keys

**Videos 23.1–23.5** The location of the keys to type the circumflex accent (^), less than (<), greater than (>), diagonal (/), and backslash (\) symbols are shown in the following diagram, and the reaches are demonstrated in Videos 23.1 through 23.5. The circumflex accent, less than symbol, and greater than symbol require the use of the left Shift key. Practice the key reaches and Shift key combinations while watching the videos.

**Exercises 23.2–23.9** Complete Exercises 23.2 through 23.6 to learn these new keys. When keying drill lines, follow the instruction prompts in the Online Lab. Work on improving your general speed and accuracy by completing Exercises 23.7 and 23.8. Finally, check your understanding of symbols by completing the Thinking Drill, Exercise 23.9.

## Accuracy Drills

For the accuracy drills, key each line once and concentrate on control as you key. After practicing the accuracy drills, go directly to Timing 10.3 to see if your accuracy has improved.

**Exercise 10.5**  Double-Letter Words Drill

Key each line once. Focus on control.

1 slipping sipping happen flipping appease shipping
2 terriers irritates terrains follow all twitter
3 dimmer dinners hammering manners immense immerges

4 moon roof pool hood hook loot took mood root door
5 gobble rabble hobble babble pebble nibbles rabbit
6 of off offers offends offset offense offering offside

7 Janelle slipped the irritated terrier in the door.
8 That immense rabbit followed and nibbled a bottle.
9 She will be shipping the poor winter winner soon.

**Exercise 10.6**  Longer Words Drill

Key each line once. Focus on control.

1 elephant dependent safekeeping plaintiff pipeline
2 standard registrar parenthesis telegrams resident
3 That resident registrar sends standard telegrams.

4 familiar eliminate sentimental dependent estimate
5 immigration minimum fumigate memorial intimidated
6 Eliminate that sentimental, familiar newspaper.

7 rational tradition imagination negotiate international
8 ambition elaborate independent establish possible
9 stalwart knowledge handwriting wholesale whenever
10 Establish rational imagination when possible.

3-Minute Timings

There is a new way to lay out a great garden that uses grids of neat 1-foot by 1-foot squares. You plant the seeds and plants with certain spacings. The system is a simple one that allows persons to make the most of a small garden space and at the same time conserve water and labor. Talented experts feel that 1-foot by 1-foot garden schemes let you grow the same amount of food as a regular garden does in less than one-fifth of the space.

 **Ergonomic Tip**

Use a desk lamp (task lighting) instead of overhead lights to eliminate screen glare.

## Ending the Session

The Online Lab automatically saved the work you completed for this session. You can continue with the next session or exit the Online Lab and continue later.

## Assessing Your Speed and Accuracy

Now that you have practiced the appropriate speed and accuracy drills, complete two 1-minute timings using the following paragraph. Note that this is the same text keyed for Timings 10.1 and 10.2.

Each timing will start as soon as you begin keying. Remember to press Tab at the start of the paragraph. If you finish keying the paragraph before the timing expires, press Enter and start keying the paragraph again.

When time expires, the Online Lab will give you a WPM rate and will show you any errors you made in the keyed text. The results of your timings will be stored in your Timings Performance report. Compare your rates from Timings 10.3 and 10.4 to your rates from Timings 10.1 and 10.2. Has your speed improved? Do you have fewer errors? If you are not meeting the WPM and error goals specified in the Online Lab, repeat Sessions 7–9.

### 1-Minute Timings

**Timings 10.3–10.4**

When the winter snow thaws, warm rain washes the world. Wild flowers begin to flutter in a slow swing with the wind. Whiffs of a meadow awakened swirl down at the dawn. The dew is a rainbow and twinkles as a jewel. Winter has blown onward.

### Success Tip

As noted, repeat Sessions 7–9 if you did not reach the timings' WPM and error goals. Without these skills, it will take you longer to master keyboarding.

### Ergonomic Tip

Focus directly on your paper copy by placing it on a document stand rather than flat on the work surface.

## Ending the Session

The Online Lab automatically saved the work you completed for this session. You can continue with the next session or exit the Online Lab and continue later.

**Exercise**
**22.10**

Reinforcement Drill

Key lines 1–9 once while concentrating on control. Press Enter after each line.

1  s2@s s@2s s2s s@s S@S S@S S@S s@s s@s s2s s@s

2  23 @ $2.31, 172 @ $8.91; 17 @ 57, 98 @ 34, 8,934 @ 90, 2 @ 4

3  dsmith@ppi-edu.com; @phantom; @boo; tmodl@ppi-edu.net

4  =; =;= =;= =;= ;=; ;=; =;= =;= ;=; ;=; = =

5  a=b c=d e=f G=J H=I K=L m=n o=p q=r

6  The = sign is used in formulas when working in spreadsheets.

7  ;+; ;=; ;+; ;=; ;+; ;=; ;+:+:=; ;=+; :=+: :+=:

8  The formula A = C + BA is the same as A = (C + BA).

9  The spreadsheet formula stated D1 = (B2 + C3 + A1) * F4.

## Assessing Your Speed and Accuracy

Complete Timings 22.1 through 22.4 in the Online Lab. Reference the paragraphs from the textbook as you key. Timings 22.3 and 22.4 use the same paragraph of text.

Each timing will start as soon as you begin keying. Remember to press Tab at the start of the paragraph. If you finish keying the paragraph before the timing expires, press Enter and start keying the paragraph again.

The Online Lab specifies the WPM and error goals. When time expires, the Online Lab will give you a WPM rate and error report for the timing. The results of the timings will be stored in your Timings Performance report.

### 1-Minute Timings

**Timing 22.1**

Symbols are used frequently in computer programming languages. Of course, the plus (+), minus (-), and equals (=) keys are used. The asterisk (*) is used as a multiplication sign, and the diagonal (introduced in the next session) is used for division. It is important that we key symbols just as quickly as we key numbers and letters.

**Timing 22.2**

Silicon Valley's technology frenzy burst onto the stock market Thursday as XYZ Corp.'s shares more than doubled in their first day of trading, setting the stage for debuts from other Internet companies in the next six months. The outsize demand for the stock of an Internet company that is growing rapidly but had a profit of $12.5 million last year is the largest sign of the surge (some say "bubble") in valuations, even as the broader US economy tries to rebound.

# Session
# 11
# V, Z, C

## Session Objectives

- **Identify the V, Z, and C keys**
- **Practice correct finger positioning for the V, Z, and C keys**
- **Explore using the correct -*ed* and -*ing* endings for verbs while keyboarding**

## Getting Started

**Exercise 11.1**  If you are continuing immediately from Session 10, you may skip the Exercise 11.1 warm-up drill. However, if you exited the Online Lab at the end of Session 10, warm up by completing Exercise 11.1.

## Introducing the V, Z, and C Keys

**Videos 11.1–11.3**  The locations of the V, Z, and C keys are shown in the following diagram. Watch Videos 11.1 through 11.3 and practice using these new keys.

**Exercises 11.2–11.10**  Complete Exercises 11.2 through 11.9 to learn these new keys. Also complete the thinking drill, Execise 11.10. When keying the drill lines, follow the instruction prompts in the Online Lab.

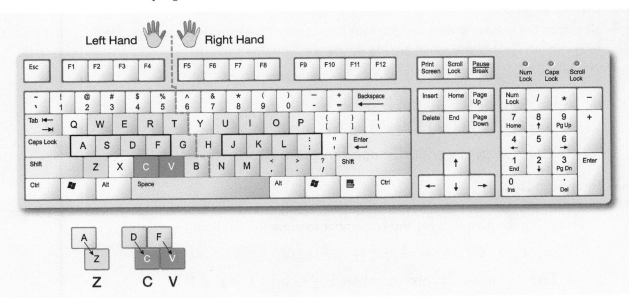

## ＷＡ Reinforcing Your Skills

Complete Exercises 22.7 through 22.10 in the Online Lab. Reference the drill lines from the textbook as you key and keep your eyes on the textbook pages, not on your fingers. Press Enter after each line. Complete each exercise at least once, but repeat exercises if you want to improve your WPM rate or accuracy.

 **Success Tip**

In the next four sets of drills, watch your finger make the reach from the home row to the symbol key the first three times you press it. Then concentrate on keeping your eyes on the text to gain speed.

**Exercise 22.7**   **At Sign Drill**

Key lines 1–5 once and then key the five lines again. Concentrate on control. Anchor the F finger when keying the at sign (@) and remember to press the right Shift key.

1 .s2s s2s s2s s2s s2s s2s s2s s@s s@s s2@s s2@s

2 14 @ $2.50, 16 @ $55.80, 1 @ $17.59, 13 @ $124.66

3 It is better to buy 99 @ 18 rather than 180 @ 10.

4 jjones@ppi-edu.com; Xavier@KU; vang@ppi-edu.net

5 @chicagotheatre.info @auditoriumtheatre.com @cnet @facebook

**Exercise 22.8**   **Equals Sign Drill**

Key lines 1–4 once and then key the four lines again. Concentrate on control. Do not use the Shift key. Anchor the J finger when keying the equals sign (=).

1 .;=; ;=; ;=; ;=; ;=; ;=; ;=; ;=; =;= =;= =;= =;= ;=

2 a = b c = d e = f g = g j = j k = k l = l ;=; ;=;;

3 A = D C = D J = J K = K L = L A = B C = D E = R =;

4 The = sign is generally used in math problems now.

**Exercise 22.9**   **Plus Sign Drill**

Key lines 1–4 once and then key the four lines again. Concentrate on control. Anchor the J finger when keying the plus sign (+) and remember to press the left Shift key.

1 ;=; ;+; ;+; ;=+; ;+:+:+=; ;=; ;+; ;=; ;+; ;=; :+;

2 The equations were: A = D + F + G and E = E + RT.

3 The equations were: A = B + C + E and H = A + BC.

4 The computer program stated A = (B + C + D) * AK.

## ﷽ Reinforcing Your Skills

Complete Exercises 11.12 through 11.15 in the Online Lab. Reference the drill lines from the textbook as you key and keep your eyes on the textbook pages, not on your fingers. Complete each exercise at least once, but repeat exercises if you want to improve your WPM rate or accuracy.

**Exercise 11.11**  V Drill

Key each drill line twice and push for speed. Try to reach 25 WPM (or the goal set by your instructor). Your WPM rate will appear after keying each line.

1  vi vim vigor vital vault vain prove provide various volume
2  love Viking violent van vote viable prove Vivian leave
3  Vermont Marvel Vernon Vitamin November Paved

Key lines 4–6 once and then key the three lines again. Concentrate on control. Try to reach 25 WPM and make two or fewer errors (or follow the goals set by your instructor). Your WPM rate will appear after keying each line, and any errors will be highlighted.

4  Vernon voted for the woman from Nevada in November.
5  Violet varnished twelve Vermont made shelves in five hours.
6  Nevada living is interesting, invigorating, and motivating.

**Exercise 11.12**  Z Drill

Key each drill line twice and push for speed. Try to reach 25 WPM (or the goal set by your instructor). Your WPM rate will appear after keying each line.

1  az maze maze doze doze raze raze zip zebra zest
2  seize breeze amaze razor hazel zombies wizard zing zane
3  Trapeze Zealous Pretzel Horizon Zealous Zenith

Key lines 4–6 once and then key the three lines again. Concentrate on control. Try to reach 25 WPM and make two or fewer errors (or follow the goals set by your instructor). Your WPM rate will appear after keying each line, and any errors will be highlighted.

4  Liz seized that sizzling pizza and ate with zeal.
5  Minimize the hazard and stabilize that bulldozer.
6  Zeb baked a dozen pretzels in the sizzling blaze.

**Exercise 11.13**  C Drill

Key each drill line twice and push for speed. Try to reach 25 WPM (or the goal set by your instructor). Your WPM rate will appear after keying each line.

1  ca calk cane case calf camp carp cave cede cad came
2  camera notice impact circle decide zinc clock corner
3  Compare Produce Consult Service Council Enclosure Carl

*drill continues*

## Session 22 — At, Equals, and Plus Signs

### Session Objectives

- Identify the at sign (@), equals sign (=), and plus sign (+) keys
- Practice correct finger positioning for the at sign (@), equals sign (=), and plus sign (+) keys

### Getting Started

**Exercise 22.1** If you are continuing immediately from Session 21, you may skip the Exercise 22.1 warm-up drill. However, if you exited the Online Lab at the end of Session 21, warm up by completing Exercise 22.1.

### Introducing the At, Equals, and Plus Sign Keys

**Videos 22.1–22.3** The location of the keys to type the at sign (@), equals sign (=), and plus sign (+) are shown in the following diagram, and the reaches are demonstrated in Videos 22.1 through 22.3. The at sign and the plus sign require the use of the Shift key. Practice the key reaches and Shift key combinations while watching the videos.

**Exercises 22.2–22.6** Complete Exercises 22.2 through 22.4 to learn these new keys. When keying the drill lines, follow the instruction prompts in the Online Lab. Work on improving your general speed and accuracy by completing Exercise 22.5. Finally, check your understanding of symbols by completing the Thinking Drill, Exercise 22.6.

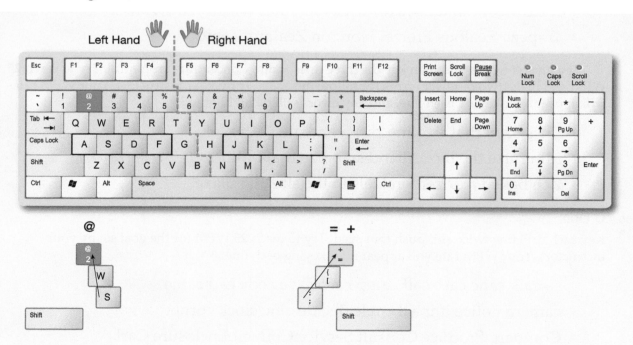

Key lines 4–6 once and then key the three lines again. Concentrate on control. Try to reach 25 WPM and make two or fewer errors (or follow the goals set by your instructor). Your WPM rate will appear after keying each line, and any errors will be highlighted.

   4 Carlton, the cat, curled in comfort in the chair.

   5 Chris decided to purchase a record and a picture.

   6 Cecelia consumed a rich chocolate ice cream cone.

**Exercise 11.14** Reinforcement Drill

Key lines 1 and 2 once for speed. Try to reach 25 WPM (or the goal set by your instructor). Your WPM rate will appear after keying each line.

   1 She loves violet vases in various rooms and on her veranda.

   2 Voices were overheard coming from the five oval offices.

Key line 3 once. Concentrate on control. Try to reach 25 WPM and make two or fewer errors (or follow the goals set by your instructor). Your WPM rate will appear after keying each line, and any errors will be highlighted.

   3 Victor was a victim of violent actions by Marv and Vernon.

 **Success Tip**

When keying for control, try to make fewer than two errors in a line. Be sure to keep your eyes on the source text in the textbook as you key.

Follow the previous procedures and key lines 4 and 5 once for speed. Key line 6 once for speed, while also concentrating on control.

   4 Hazel won the prize as Buzz gazed with amazement.

   5 The freezing drizzle glazed the bronze zinnias.

   6 Hal has been penalized after embezzling a zillion.

Follow the previous procedures and key lines 7 and 8 once for speed. Key line 9 once for speed, while also concentrating on control.

   7 With tonic and citric acid, can Carrie cure colds?

   8 Could the clever client conceal crucial evidence?

   9 A crow circled the cottage as Vivian watched with caution.

**Ergonomic Tip**

Rest your forearms on the edge of a table. Grasp the fingers of one hand and gently bend your wrist back for five seconds to relax your hand and fingers.

## Ending the Session

The Online Lab automatically saved the work you completed for this session. You can continue with the next session or exit the Online Lab and continue later.

# Assessing Your Speed and Accuracy

Complete Timings 11.1 through 11.6 in the Online Lab to assess the skills you have learned in this session. Refer to the following paragraphs as you key.

Each timing will start as soon as you begin keying. Remember to press Tab at the start of the paragraph. If you finish keying the paragraph before the timing expires, press Enter and start keying the paragraph again.

The Online Lab specifies WPM and error goals. When time expires, the Online Lab will give you a WPM rate and will show you any errors you made in the keyed text. The results will be stored in your Timings Performance report.

## 1-Minute Timings

**Timing 11.1**

Traveling in this vast, native land is a near marvel. The savage rivers and various paved miles are impressive. Vivid sights revive the mind and lift spirits. Villages reveal veiled vestiges; a dividend is derived.

**Timing 11.2**

Even if Viola is vain, she has avid fans and attentive friends. Her singing is sensitive; she reveals her vast talent. She deserves lavish and vivid praise. Her versatile verses are a massive advantage and elevate her fevered fans.

**Timing 11.3**

Zeb zipped to that zoo with zest and nuzzled the zebras. He sneezed in the breeze and went to see the lizards. He wants to be a zoologist when he gets older. He knows a zillion things, and his dazed and puzzled parents are amazed.

**Timing 11.4**

Zelda gazed in amazement as Zip, the wizard, seized a wand. It was ablaze with a maze of fire and lights. He did dozens of hazardous feats and puzzled all at the bazaar. He also was a trapeze whiz and dazzled folks.

**Timing 11.5**

A cookout on the beach could include cheese, carrots, meat sandwiches, and cold juice. If the chill of the ocean is too much, hot chocolate and hot coffee can chase the cold chills. The decent lunch and a chat with chums can enrich affection.

**Timing 11.6**

An office clerk who lacks basic ethics could become the subject of scorn. Those persisting in cruel and careless attacks on certain new workers can cause havoc. It is logical to follow strict, concise rules concerning office tact. Choose the right track and be sincere.

# Assessing Your Speed and Accuracy

Complete Timings 21.1 through 21.4 in the Online Lab. Refer to the following paragraphs as you key. Timings 21.3 and 21.4 use the same paragraph of text.

Each timing will start as soon as you begin keying. Remember to press Tab at the start of the paragraph. If you finish keying the paragraph before the timing expires, press Enter and start keying the paragraph again.

The Online Lab specifies the WPM and error goals. When time expires, the Online Lab will give you a WPM rate and error report for the timing. The results of the timings will be stored in your Timings Performance report.

### 1-Minute Timings

**Timing 21.1**

The stock market gets a lot of people's attention. When Standard & Poor's index increases, many people will hold on to their stocks in anticipation of further gains. A 4% drop in durable goods orders would most likely increase short-term interest rates; this has an impact on the Federal Reserve Board's next move.

**Timing 21.2**

While walking on the 200 block of West Division Street on the afternoon of July 31, 2016, a 26-year-old man was approached by an unknown man believed to be in his fifties who asked if he was disabled. The man answered that he was, and the stranger told him to hand over five dollars. The man then took out his wallet, which contained $17 in cash, and the offender snatched it from him. A foot chase ensured, and the two fought in a parking lot until the offender agreed to give the wallet and money back.

### 3-Minute Timings

**Timings 21.3–21.4**

The first-of-its-kind building features 248 spacious and elegant one-, two-, and three-bedroom apartments that offer nine floor plans with dramatic views of the cityscape. The apartments offer everything you need to feel comfortable, relaxed, and positive about life. Though they come standard with a range of high-end amenities and thoughtful details, custom amenities and features are available to reflect your personal sense of style. All apartments have full state-of-the-art kitchens, washers and dryers, and floor-to-ceiling windows with panoramic views. Fast elevator service connects residents to several floors and well-appointed, warm, and inviting common areas. These levels include a spa, fitness center, and pool. On the fifty-third floor is a gathering spot with awesome views of the city and lake. Floor plans are available for viewing now and will go on sale April 2021.

**Ergonomic Tip**

Position your document stand about the same distance from your eyes as the screen to avoid refocusing for different distances.

## Ending the Session

The Online Lab automatically saved the work you completed for this session. You can continue with the next session or exit the Online Lab and continue later.

**Success Tip**

In the next two drills, watch your little finger make the reach the first three times you key the left and right brackets. Then look at the text for the remainder of the drill.

**Exercise 21.14   Left Bracket Drill**

Key lines 1 and 2 for speed. Key lines 1 and 2 a second time while focusing on control. Do not use the Shift key. Anchor the J finger when making this reach.

1   ;[; ;[; ;[; ;[; ;[; ;[; ;[[ ;[[ ;[; ;[[; ;[[;

2   ;[ ;[ ;[ ;[; ;[[; ;[[; ;[ ;[[; ;[[; ;[; ;[[;

**Exercise 21.15   Left and Right Brackets Drill**

Key lines 1 and 2 and then key the two lines again. Focus on control.

1   ;[; ;]; ;[; ;]; ;[; ;]; ;]; ;[; ;]; ;[; ;[; ;]];

2   ;[ ]; ;[; ;]; ;[; [;] [;] [;] [;] [;] [;] [;] [;]

**Exercise 21.16   Reinforcement Drill**

Key the following drill lines once. Press Enter after each line.

1   k* K*K k*k k8*k k8k*k k*k*k k8*k k8*k k*k K*K k*k

2   The * symbol is used in formulas: A1 * B2 - C2 * 49.

3   f%f f5%f f%f f5%5 f5%f f5%f f5%f f%5f 5%5 5%5 555

4   Did you know that 5% of 5,000 equals 250% of 100?

5   ;[;[; ;[;[; ;[;[[ ;[;[ ;[; ;[; ;[; ;[; ;[;; ;[; ;[;

6   ;];]; ;]; ;]; ;]; ;];]; ;]; ];]; ];]; ;]; ;]; ;]; ;]];

7   [;] [;] [;] [;] [;] [;] [;] [;] ;]; ;]; ;]; ;[; ;[ ;]

8   ;[; ;]; ;]; ;[; ;[; ;]; ;]; ;[; ;]; ;[; ;[; ;]; ;[; ;];

9   l9 l(l l9L1 l9(l l(l l9(l l9(l l9l l9l l(l l(l

10   ;); ;0); ;0); ;0); ;); ;0); ;); ;); ;); ;); ;);(0)

11   The amount ($6.96) was more ($2 more) than I paid.

12   Most of the table (see Table 3.2) was accurate.

## Session
# 12
# Y, X, Q

### Session Objectives

- **Identify the Y, X, and Q keys**
- **Practice correct finger positioning for the Y, X, and Q keys**

---

## Getting Started

**Exercise 12.1**    If you are continuing immediately from Session 11, you may skip the Exercise 12.1 warm-up drill. However, if you exited the Online Lab at the end of Session 11, warm up by completing Exercise 12.1.

## Introducing the Y, X, and Q Keys

**Videos 12.1–12.3**    The locations of the Y, X, and Q keys are shown in the following diagram. Watch Videos 12.1 through 12.3 and practice using these new keys.

**Exercises 12.2–12.10**    Complete Exercises 12.2 through 12.9 to learn these new keys. Also complete the thinking drill, Exercise 12.10. When keying the drill lines, follow the instruction prompts in the Online Lab.

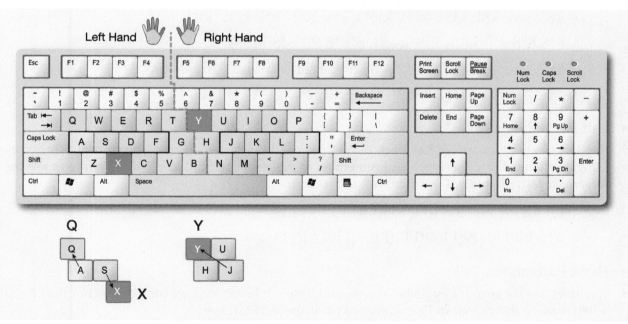

## ⋙ Reinforcing Your Skills

Complete Exercises 21.10 through 21.16 in the Online Lab. Reference the drill lines from the textbook as you key and keep your eyes on the textbook pages, not on your fingers. Press Enter after each line. Complete each exercise at least once, but repeat exercises if you want to improve your WPM rate or accuracy.

**Exercise 21.10** Percent Sign Drill

Place both hands on the home row and practice the reach from the F key to the percent sign key. Be sure to anchor your left little finger to the A key and remember to press the right Shift key.

Key lines 1–4 for speed. Key lines 1–4 a second time while focusing on control.

1 f5f f5f f5f f5f f5f f%f F%F f5f F%F5 f%f5 f%f f%f

2 55% 555% 5% 5%5% 555% 55% 5% 5% 55% 555% 5%, 555%

3 A 6% discount and a 10% reduction will equal 16%.

4 They made 55% of their shots and 8% of the fouls.

**Exercise 21.11** Asterisk Drill

In addition to signaling a footnote or indicating spacing, the asterisk serves as a multiplication sign in some programming languages. Anchor the J finger to make the reach to the asterisk key and remember to press the left Shift key.

Key lines 1–4 for speed. Key lines 1–4 a second time while focusing on control. Remember to press the left Shift key.

1 k8k k8k k8k ki8k ki8k ki8*k k*k K*K k*k k*k *ki*k

2 8*8 8*8 8*8 k8*k ki8*k k*k 8*8*8 *** 8*8 ki8* k*k

3 The check was for $***4.65 and it should be $46.50.

4 The * symbol is used in programming: A - B * 38.

**Exercise 21.12** Left Parenthesis Drill

Key lines 1 and 2 for speed. Key lines 1 and 2 a second time while focusing on control. Anchor the J finger when making this reach and remember to press the left Shift key. *Note: Be sure to use the lowercase letter L and not the number 1 in this drill.*

1 l9l l9l l9l l9l lo9l lo9l lo9(l l(l l(l lo(l lo9(

2 l(l l(l l(l l9l l9l l9(l lo9(l lo(l lo9(l l9Ll l(l l9

**Exercise 21.13** Right Parenthesis Drill

Key lines 1–4 for speed. Key lines 1–4 a second time while focusing on control. Anchor the J finger when making this reach. and remember to press the left Shift key.

1 ;0; ;0; ;0; ;0; ;p0; ;p0; ;p0; ;p0; ;p); ;p); ;0;

2 ;); ;); ;); ;); ;); ;0); ;); ;0); ;p0); ;p0); ;);

3 The price ($5.95) was more ($2 more) than I paid.

4 Most of the teams (at least 6) won all six games.

## ⤳⤳ Reinforcing Your Skills

Complete Exercises 12.11 through 12.14 in the Online Lab. Reference the drill lines from the textbook as you key and keep your eyes on the textbook pages, not on your fingers. Complete each exercise at least once, but repeat exercises if you want to improve your WPM rate or accuracy.

**Exercise 12.11**  Y Drill

Key each drill line twice and push for speed. Try to reach 25 WPM (or the goal set by your instructor). Your WPM rate will appear after keying each line.

1 jy yard play yowl very yolk away lazy sly yield you tube
2 spray dairy entry handy lucky staying yonder young
3 Yearn Decay Empty Forty Hurry Lousy Playing Yale Taylor

Key lines 4–6 once and then key the three lines again. Concentrate on control. Try to reach 25 WPM and make two or fewer errors (or follow the goals set by your instructor). Your WPM rate will appear after keying each line, and any errors will be highlighted.

4 The kitty and the puppy may not enjoy happy play.
5 It is only your duty to obey every law of safety.
6 Billy is ready to carry the heavy load Wednesday.

**Exercise 12.12**  X Drill

Key each drill line twice and push for speed. Try to reach 25 WPM (or the goal set by your instructor). Your WPM rate will appear after keying each line.

1 sx axle next exam flex text hoax apex expedite fix fox
2 deluxe excise expand export prefix excite text messaging
3 Explode Exhaust Examine Anxiety Exporting X ray Expert

Key lines 4–6 once and then key the three lines again. Concentrate on control. Try to reach 25 WPM and make two or fewer errors (or follow the goals set by your instructor). Your WPM rate will appear after keying each line, and any errors will be highlighted.

4 Did excess oxygen explode during that experiment?
5 Explain the context and expedite that experiment.
6 Fix the exhaust and examine the axle of the taxi.

**Exercise 12.13**  Q Drill

Key each drill line twice and push for speed. Try to reach 25 WPM (or the goal set by your instructor). Your WPM rate will appear after keying each line.

1 aq quote quire squid quiet squat query qualify quite
2 quench equate squeak equity squelching quit quartz
3 Squire Quarry Quiver Quorum Quartering Requesting

*drill continues*

# Session 21
# Percent Sign, Asterisk, Parentheses, Brackets

## Session Objectives

- **Identify the percent sign (%), asterisk (*), ( ), and [ ] keys**
- **Practice correct finger positioning for the percent sign (%), asterisk (*), ( ), and [ ] keys**

## Getting Started

**Exercise 21.1** If you are continuing immediately from Session 20, you may skip the Exercise 21.1 warm-up drill. However, if you exited the Online Lab at the end of Session 20, warm up by completing Exercise 21.1.

## Introducing the Percent Sign, the Asterisk, Parentheses, and Bracket Symbols

**Videos 21.1–21.6** The location of the keys to type the percent sign (%) and asterisk (*), left and right parentheses, and left and right brackets are shown in the following diagram, and the reaches are demonstrated in Videos 21.1 through 21.6. All of the keys except the left and right bracket keys require the use of a Shift key. Practice the key reaches and Shift key combinations while watching the videos.

**Exercises 21.2–21.9** Complete Exercises 21.2 through 21.7 to learn these new keys. When keying the drill lines, follow the instruction prompts in the Online Lab. Work on improving your general speed and accuracy by completing Exercise 21.8. Finally, check your understanding of symbols by completing the Thinking Drill, Exercise 21.9.

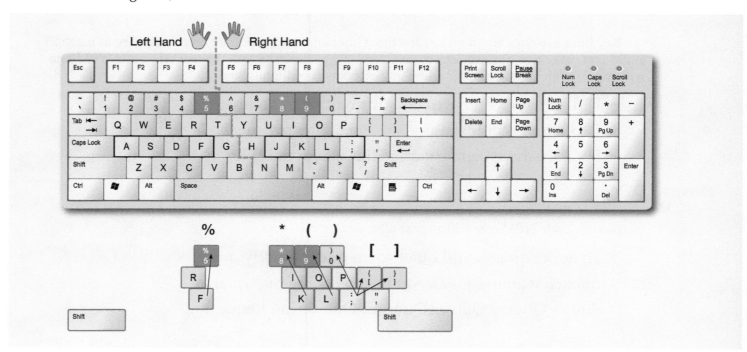

Key lines 4–6 once and then key the three lines again. Concentrate on control. Try to reach 25 WPM and make two or fewer errors (or follow the goals set by your instructor). Your WPM rate will appear after keying each line, and any errors will be highlighted.

4 Do that quotient; it is a frequent quiz question.

5 Ducks squirmed and quacked in the squalid quarry.

6 Does the quitter frequently squabble and quibble?

**Exercise 12.14** Reinforcement Drill

Key lines 1 and 2 once for speed. Try to reach 25 WPM (or the goal set by your instructor). Your WPM rate will appear after keying each line.

1 In a sunny yard, the sassy gray puppy plays daily.

2 The friendly young boy, Gary, annoys silly Sally.

Key line 3 once. Concentrate on control. Try to reach 25 WPM and make two or fewer errors (or follow the goals set by your instructor). Your WPM rate will appear at the end of the line, and any errors made will be highlighted.

3 A hungry baby in the subway was eyed by a sentry.

 **Success Tip**

When keying for control, try to make fewer than two errors in a line. Remember to keep your eyes on the textbook as you key.

Follow the previous procedures and key lines 4 and 5 once for speed. Key line 6 once for speed, while also concentrating on control.

4 Examine her next; Maxine was exposed to smallpox.

5 The new relaxing exercise was explained in the textbook.

6 Is the lynx a vexing jinx or is it an exotic pet?

Follow the previous procedures and key lines 7 and 8 once for speed. Key line 9 once for speed, while also concentrating on control.

7 The unique antique aquarium had a thick lacquer on it.

8 In the old square, the quake left a queen in a quagmire.

9 The queasy squirrel was quarantined in the square box.

3-Minute Timings

**Timings**
20.3–20.4

Why should seat belts be fastened when a car is moving? Seat belts will reduce injuries and deaths. Many tests and studies have been done to prove this point. Half of all the traffic deaths happen within 25 miles from home. Traffic deaths can occur when an auto is moving just 40 miles per hour or less. If a car is moving at 30 miles per hour, the impact is like hitting the ground after hurtling from the top of a building that is three stories high.

### Ergonomic Tip

If you are experiencing eye pain, flashes of light, eye floaters (spots in your vision), blind spots, or blurred vision, make an appointment immediately with a qualified professional.

## Ending the Session

The Online Lab automatically saved the work you completed for this session. You can continue with the next session or exit the Online Lab and continue later.

## Assessing Your Speed and Accuracy

Complete Timings 12.1 through 12.6 in the Online Lab to assess the skills you have learned in this session. Refer to the following paragraphs as you key.

Each timing will start as soon as you begin keying. Remember to press Tab at the beginning of the paragraph. If you finish keying the paragraph before the timing expires, press Enter and start keying the paragraph again.

The Online Lab specifies WPM and error goals. When the time expires, the Online Lab will give you a WPM rate and will highlight any errors you made in the keyed text. The results will be stored in your Timings Performance report.

### 1-Minute Timings

**Timing 12.1**
Basically, employers like a loyal employee. Honesty and courtesy always pay off in any job or duty. Apathy and sloppy typing are always likely to be very costly to a company. Any employee who displays a steady style will be properly rewarded and enjoy a fairly large salary.

**Timing 12.2**
There is simply no key to easy money. A bad agency may say that you are lucky and a legacy of wealthy glory is yours. Yet, if you try fancy or phony schemes, you will be mighty sorry. Steady, weekly saving is the thrifty means to easy money. Lay a penny away a day and be happy.

**Timing 12.3**
An extra exercise to help your mind relax is inhaling and exhaling deeply. It extends all the oxygen capacity before it is expelled. Choose an exact time each day to expedite an extra relaxing exertion. Your anxieties and vexations disappear and you relax. Try this excellent experience.

**Timing 12.4**
Exercise an extreme caution before investing in an old duplex. Have an expert examine all the existing details and explain them to you. It may be easier to buy a luxurious and deluxe apartment house. An experienced land expert knows if it is an expensive venture.

**Timing 12.5**
The quick squad conquered the unique quintet without question. The quarterback squelched most questions about technique or quality of the team. If they qualify for the trophy, will they quietly squash the next team, or will the coach require an extra practice session?

**Timing 12.6**
Angelique might request a price quotation on an exquisite antique quilt. She acquired it from a queen in a quaint town near the equator. Quiet inquiries have arisen from qualified buyers. The question is, should she keep the quality quilt or sell it quickly, as requested?

7 j7j j7j& j&j& j&j& j7j7 &&& j& j& j7 j& j& j7j7

8 &j& j7j& j&j& && j7j& j7& &&77 77 &7 &7 7&7& 777

9 Patricia and Ron went to Samuelsons & Bigsby today.

10 a!a! a!a a!a a!a! a! a! a!a! a!a a!a a!a a! a! a!

11 What! How frightening! Mark your calendar!

12 My brother yelled, "Run for your life!" Wow!

## Assessing Your Speed and Accuracy

Complete Timings 20.1 through 20.4 in the Online Lab. Refer to the following paragraphs as you key. Timings 20.3 and 20.4 use the same paragraph.

Each timing will start as soon as you begin keying. Remember to press Tab at the start of the paragraph. If you finish keying the paragraph before the timing expires, press Enter and start keying the paragraph again.

The Online Lab specifies the WPM and error goals. When the time expires, the Online Lab will give you a WPM rate and error report for the timing. The results of the timings will be stored in your Timings Performance report.

### 1-Minute Timings

**Timing 20.1**

State, county, and regional fairs provide wholesome entertainment for more than 150 million Americans each year. The Texas State Fair has an annual $60 million impact on the Dallas-Fort Worth area with more than 1.5 million attendees. From animals to high-tech displays, there's something for everyone, and the price is right!

**Timing 20.2**

When ordering team jerseys, be sure to include #223-852 in the category box on the order form. JB & K provides an additional 15 percent discount for orders in excess of 25 jerseys. There is a significant savings on two-color jerseys compared to those with three or more colors. Prices are listed on the attached sheet.

 **Success Tip**

Try to increase your speed while maintaining accuracy.

 **Ergonomic Tip**

Adjust the brightness and contrast controls on the screen to make text and images easier to see.

## Ending the Session

The Online Lab automatically saved the work you completed for this session. You can continue with the next session or exit the Online Lab and continue later.

### Exercise 20.8 — Exclamation Point Drill

Key the following drill lines once. Space once after each exclamation point (except at the end of a line). Remember to press the right Shift key.

1 Help! Stop! No! Yes! Go! Wait! Begin! Halt! None!

2 Walter, stop right now! You had all better stop!

3 No, you cannot go right now! Listen to them now!

### Exercise 20.9 — Pound and Number Sign Drill

Key the following drill lines once. Concentrate on control. Remember to press the right Shift key.

1 #33 33# 39 9# #168 168# #106 106# #3 3#3 21# #122

2 Items #10, #7, #3, #6, #4, #12, and #19 are mine.

3 Get #61 weighing 10# and #2299 weighing 189,756#.

### Exercise 20.10 — Dollar Sign Drill

Key the following drill lines once. Concentrate on control. Remember to press the right Shift key.

1 $1 $2 $3 $4 $5 $6 $7 $8 $9 $10 $11 $120 $16.00 f$

2 Add $1.16, $28.96, $17.44, $18.00, $21.13, $4.26.

3 The gifts cost $1.10, $6.90, $19.89, and $101.13.

### Exercise 20.11 — Ampersand Drill

Key the following drill lines once. Concentrate on control. Remember to press the left Shift key.

1 17 & 60 & 9 & 16 & 14 & 71 & 77 & 45 & 61 & 9891

2 Buy gifts from the J & K store and also R & Sons.

3 Contact Hart & Sole for the products you need.

### Exercise 20.12 — Reinforcement Drill

Key the following drill lines once. Concentrate on control.  Remember to press the right Shift key.

1 f$f$f f4f f$f$ f$f$ f4f4 $$$ f$ f$ f4 f$ f$ f4 f4

2 $40.00 4$ $4.00 $$44 $4.00 $$44 44 $4 $4 f$f$ 444

3 $143,789.00 $1,640.68 $689.33 $17.31 $26.80 $1.44

4 d#d d3d# d#d# d#d# d3d3 ### d# d# d3 d# d# d3 d3

5 d#d d3#d #3 3# ##33 3# #3 ##33 33 #3 #3 3#3# 333

6 Buy 14#, 23#, 71#, 3#, 8#, 41#, 13#, 21#, and 6#.

*drill continues*

# Session 13

# Skills Reinforcement and Proficiency Exercises: Sessions 1–12

## ⚐ Session Objectives

- **Review and practice correct finger positioning for the keys learned in Sessions 1–12**
- **Assess and reinforce keyboarding speed and accuracy with timings**
- **Utilize drills to practice alphabetic keying**

## Getting Started

**Exercise 13.1**   If you are continuing immediately from Session 12, you may skip the warm-up drill at the start of this session. However, if you exited the Online Lab at the end of Session 12, warm up by completing Exercise 13.1.

The purpose of this session is to reinforce the keyboarding skills you have developed in the previous sessions. The timings in this session will help you to determine where you are in your skill development, and the exercises in the session provide you with the opportunity to further work on improving your skill and accuracy.

## Assessing Your Speed and Accuracy

In Sessions 7–9 and 11–12, you completed a series of 1-minute timings. The speed and accuracy goals were presented with each set of timings in the Online Lab. Check your scores by accessing your Timings Performance report.

Using your scores for the timings in Sessions 7–9 and 11–12 as benchmarks, complete Timings 13.1 and 13.2 in the Online Lab using the paragraph at the top of the next page. If you did not meet the WPM goals in the previous timings, push for speed. If you reached the WPM goals but did not meet the error goals, work on accuracy. If you achieved both the speed and accuracy goals, push for even greater speed.

In the Online Lab, you will start with a practice screen, which you can use to practice keying the timing text without the timer. Prompt the Online Lab to begin Timing 13.1 when you have completed your practice. Both timings use the same paragraph. Once you are on an active timing screen, the timing will start as soon as you begin keying.

Remember to press Tab at the start of the paragraph. Also, do not press Enter at the end of each line, but only at the end of the paragraph. If you finish keying the paragraph before the timing expires, press Enter and start keying the paragraph again.

The Online Lab specifies WPM and error goals. When the time expires, the Online Lab will give you a WPM rate and highlight any errors you made in the keyed text. The results of both timings will be stored in your Timings Performance report.

## Correctly Using the Exclamation Point

The exclamation point is used to express a high degree of emotion or strong feeling. As with other end-of-sentence punctuation, you should key only one space after an exclamation point when it ends a sentence (unless it is at the end of a paragraph). Review the following examples before completing Exercise 20.7.

> No way! You mean the flight has been delayed for six hours?
> How frightening! The fire broke out only 10 minutes after we left.
> The date of the meeting—mark it on your calendar!—is November 10.
> So there you are, rascal!
> My brother yelled, "Run for your life!"
> I simply do not believe the fiscal report that states, "The absentee rate was increasing by 500 percent"!

**Exercise 20.7** Exclamation Point Drill

Key the missing punctuation as you key the following drill lines. If the punctuation is missing or misplaced in the keyed text, the Online Lab will indicate the error. Press Enter at the end of each line. *Hint: In one instance, you also need to add the proper punctuation for a quotation. Review the section "Quotation Marks with Other Punctuation Symbols" in Session 19, page 98, if necessary.*

1 Congratulations, you won the first prize

2 Jan shouted What a mess

3 I emphatically restate my position: I will not fire those workers

4 Help Help I'm locked in this room.

5 Oh, how ridiculous He's never even seen the inside of a bank?

## Correctly Using the Pound and Dollar Signs

The pound sign (#) is also commonly referred to as the *number sign*. (In a social-media context, this symbol is sometimes referred to as a "hash symbol" or "hashtag.") When the symbol appears before a number, it is read as "number." For example, *item #10* would be read as "item number ten." When the symbol follows a number, it is read as "pound" or "pounds." For example, *buy 3#* would be read as "buy three pounds." In either instance, do not insert a space between the number and the symbol.

## Correctly Using the Ampersand

The ampersand (&) is equivalent to the word "and." When an ampersand is used within a line of text, key one space before and one space after the symbol.

## Reinforcing Your Skills

Complete Exercises 20.8 through 20.12 in the Online Lab. Reference the drill lines from the textbook as you key and keep your eyes on the textbook pages, not on your fingers. Press Enter after each line. Complete each exercise at least once, but repeat exercises if you want to improve your WPM rate or accuracy.

## 1-Minute Timings

Timings
13.1–13.2

It is good to have honest goals. Nothing is gained if one goes forth in pointless roaming. A major effort is needed to prosper. Isolate those foolish errors and avoid them. Hold to a strong, firm hope and move along.

# Reinforcing Your Skills

The following key-location, speed, and accuracy drills provide additional practice on the keys you have learned in the previous sessions. If you successfully keyed Timings 13.1 and 13.2 and met or exceeded the goals specified in the Online Lab, proceed to Session 14. However, if your WPM and error rates do not match these goals, the drills in this section will give you the opportunity for further practice.

If you have not mastered a key reach (you hesitate before striking a key), practice the alphabetic key location drills, Exercises 13.2 through 13.4. If you are not meeting the WPM goals, key the speed drills, Exercises 13.5 through 13.7. If you are committing more errors than specified in the Online Lab, key the accuracy drills, Exercises 13.8 and 13.9.

## Alphabetic Key Location Drills

Practice the following drills to help reinforce your keying of the alphabetic characters. Repeat these exercises as often as you like to help you increase both your speed and accuracy.

**Exercise 13.2   Key Positioning Drill**

Practice the correct finger position on the home row keys by keying each letter of the alphabet twice with one space between each letter set (aa bb cc dd and so on).

**Exercise 13.3   Key Positioning Thinking Drill**

Develop your critical thinking skills when keyboarding by keying the alphabet backwards with one space between each letter (z y x and so on).

**Exercise 13.4   Alphabetic Characters Sentence Drill**

Key the following sentence three times to practice keying all of the letters of the alphabet.

1 The quick brown fox jumped over the lazy dogs.

## Speed Drills

For the speed drills, key each line once. After practicing the speed drills, either continue by completing the accuracy drills or go directly to Timing 13.3 to see if your speed has improved.

# Session 20

# Exclamation Point, Pound Sign, Dollar Sign, Ampersand

## Session Objectives

- Identify the exclamation point (!), pound sign (#), dollar sign ($), and ampersand (&) keys
- Practice correct finger positioning for the exclamation point (!), pound sign (#), dollar sign ($), and ampersand (&) keys
- Apply guidelines for use of the exclamation mark

---

## Getting Started

**Exercise 20.1**    If you are continuing immediately from Session 19, you may skip the Exercise 20.1 warm-up drill. However, if you exited the Online Lab at the end of Session 19, warm up by completing Exercise 20.1.

## Introducing the Exclamation Point, Pound Sign, Dollar Sign, and Ampersand Keys

**Videos 20.1–20.4**    The exclamation point (!), pound sign (#), dollar sign ($), and ampersand (&) are all located on the number key row. These symbols are produced by pressing the appropriate key along with a Shift key. The locations and correct finger reaches for these keys are shown in the following diagram and in Videos 20.1 through 20.4. Watch these videos and practice keying these symbols.

**Exercises 20.2–20.6**    Complete Exercises 20.2 through 20.5 to learn these new keys. When keying the drill lines, follow the instruction prompts in the Online Lab. Work on improving your general speed and accuracy by completing Exercise 20.6.

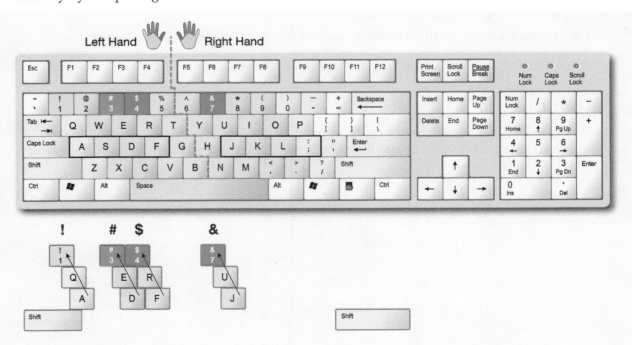

**Exercise 13.5** Balanced-Hand Words Drill

Key each line once. Focus on speed.

1 sign and the sigh ant sit ale elf hen end she and
2 then hang the and fig dig die tie did sit fit aid
3 fish sign than then lane lake lens hand than halt

4 lake idle half lens lane sign dish sign then disk
5 aisle island handle fight angle title shake snake
6 gland sleigh height fight slant digit angle eight

7 he and the elf and it if he an tight giant signal
8 amble bible problem blame bland blend lamb emblem
9 gown wig bow wow vow down wit when wish with wisp

10 flap pane paid pale spent dispel lap nap pen paid
11 foam fork form foal odor soak rod fog sod oak rod
12 heir lair risks sir pan air widow flair hair pair

13 pelvis disown pens laps vie via pair vivid flames
14 map mane maid melt sham lame mend firm make disks
15 The pale maid paid for the vivid title and a wig.

16 Did the pale lamb amble down to the big, bland pen?
17 When did Bob sign the pair of problem emblems?

**Exercise 13.6** Letter Combinations Drill

Key each line once. Focus on speed.

1 ta tall tan task taste tale take talk tag talent
2 th thesis thin theft this think than that then throw
3 te tenant tend tell tenth test tea tenor team text

4 st stead steal steadiness stateside stag steam
5 sa sad saline Sal sang said sale sake safe sat sake
6 si since simple sinker sit single sift sip sin siphon

7 pe pets pest pen peg pea peat penguin pension
8 pi pine pink pipes piles pie pin pious pint

*drill continues*

**Timing**
**19.2**

A personal computer's components determine the limitations. For example, a computer without a video card and proper video "codecs" wouldn't be able to play the content created via a GoPro camera. What can be done with the right components in today's microcomputers is amazing. It wouldn't take long to think of 101 things that could be done on a computer with the "right" components.

3-Minute Timings

**Timings**
**19.3–19.4**

Fair time is near. Last year, our county had a great fair. Lots of people came to see the fine views and have a good time. Just imagine that 539,437 people attended, which was a record. We are hoping that by the next year we can have over 600,000 at the fair. The new rides were colorful and exciting. Both the young and old had a great time. We hope that the same old amusement company will come back and bring some of those new rides and fun shows that are bigger and better.

 Ergonomic Tip

Clean your monitor regularly with an antistatic screen cleaner recommended by the monitor's manufacturer.

## Ending the Session

The Online Lab automatically saved the work you completed for this session. You can continue with the next session or exit the Online Lab and continue later.

9 li like linkage linking link lien lied lie lid lime

10 le leaf least ledge lend lead left lest leap legacy

11 bl blade bleak blast blank blinds blind blight blog

12 ba bandages barks badge bath balk bail bag bad band

13 mi mire misting might midst mint mind milk mid

14 ma margin manager marsh mail make math mat man

15 oa float roast toad load oatmeal oath oats oak boat

16 ri rinse rigid ridges right ripe rises rip rid rice

17 ra rapid range raised rates rake ranks rap ran rayon

18 vi vintage vital visits vine vile vise vim vie viable

19 va vanish varied valid vast vases vane vat van varnish

20 wa waves waste wane wait wade wag war was wash wand

21 wi wiper wield wise will wipe wide wig wit win window

**Exercise 13.7** Sentences with Letter Combinations Drill
Key each line once. Focus on speed.

1 Janie washed and wiped her wig; she wasted water.

2 The boy blinked at a baby bound in bandages.

3 Those offensive oats floated off of that oatmeal.

4 The vital vintage vases vanished from a vast van.

5 The manager might mail the mild mints to the man.

6 Rapid Red ran to the raised ridges on that range.

7 That person had piles of pipes for them.

8 Then that steady tenant, Ted, did a tenth strength test.

9 Steadfast Stacy talks a lot and stands as she talks.

10 Sad Sal sang a signal as she sighted a safe date.

11 At least lower the left lid and shorten the length.

12 That hanging kite tail brings the person around.

13 Gal, finish the gasket for the gas gadget game.

14 I dislike the heat dial that fits the dental fan.

5 The poem entitled Barney's Revenge is not very long.

6 At midnight, Joan saw The Light of Laughter on television.

7 The author's last short story, Bars on the Doors, was a mystery.

8 Her favorite song is Thunder Serenade by Mario Zahn.

**Exercise 19.8** Reinforcement Drill

Key the following drill lines once. Press the Enter key after each line.

1 ;'; ;'u';u' u'; ; ; '; u';u' u'; ; ;

2 can't couldn't John's hat, people's voice, anybody's guess

3 Donne's sonnets, girls' clothes, 100', 255', they're, it's

4 ;";" ; " ;";" ;";u" ;" ; ; ;";u";u';u" ;" ;" ;

5 "The weather is really nasty," said Nancy.

6 When did you say, "I shall not return"?

7 She asked, "Do you know if the train is late?"

8 "The Midnight Ride of Paul Revere" is a good poem.

9 My grandfather said the concert was "far out" and enjoyable.

## Assessing Your Speed and Accuracy

Complete Timings 19.1 through 19.4 in the Online Lab. Refer to the following paragraphs from the textbook as you key. Timings 19.3 and 19.4 use the same paragraph of text.

Each timing will start as soon as you begin keying. Remember to press Tab at the start of the paragraph. If you finish keying the paragraph before time expires, press Enter and start keying the paragraph again.

The Online Lab specifies the WPM and error goals. When time expires, the Online Lab will give you a WPM rate and error report for the timing. The results of the timings will be stored in your Timings Performance report.

### 1-Minute Timings

**Timing 19.1**

This new book on soccer has an excellent chapter on coaching soccer that offers 14 "awesome" tips to be used in working with young people new to the sport. There are some excellent suggestions on how to get positive support from the parents of the players. It's a great resource for coaches and their assistants.

## Accuracy Drills

For the accuracy drills, key each line once and concentrate on control as you key. After practicing the accuracy drills, go directly to Timing 13.3 to see if your accuracy has improved.

**Exercise 13.8** Double-Letter Words Drill

Key each line once. Focus on accuracy.

1 seed teens needless feeling indeed needs glee see
2 tall stall knitting install little shall hall all
3 heel steed likeness dissent seeing sheet need fee

4 see feel teeth indeed gallant sledding sleet knee
5 hill still lifeless endless assist stiff kiss add
6 eggs stall eggshell falling haggle sniff sell egg

7 tell shell settling skilled allied skill fell add
8 deed sleek seedling fiddles needle sheen keen eel
9 rabble rabbit gobble nibbles pebble babble hobble

10 narratives all follow terrains irritates terriers
11 door root mood took loot hook hood pool roof moon
12 immerges immense manners hammering dinners dimmer

13 shipping appease flipping happen sipping slipping
14 of offensive offense offset offends offers off of
15 She will be stalling the nice contest winner now.

16 That immense rabbit emerged and nibbled a carrot.
17 Tu Wee slipped the irritated kitten into the house.

**Exercise 13.9** Longer Words Drill

Key each line once. Focus on accuracy.

1 negative retrieve primitive privilege advertising
2 estimate familiar eliminate dependent sentimental
3 Eliminate that sentimental, familiar advertising.

4 resident standard telegrams registrar parenthesis
5 pipeline elephant dependent plaintiff safekeeping
6 That resident registrar sends standard telegrams.

*drill continues*

## Reinforcing Your Skills

Complete Exercises 19.6 through 19.8 in the Online Lab. For Exercises 19.6 and 19.7, you will need to key the missing quotation marks as you key the drill lines. If quotation marks are missing or misplaced in the text you key, the Online Lab will indicate the error. Exercise 19.8 is a reinforcement drill. Remember to keep your eyes on the textbook pages, not on your fingers, as you key these exercises. Complete each exercise at least once, but repeat exercises if you want to improve your WPM rate or accuracy.

**Exercise 19.6** Quotation Marks for Conversations Drill

Key the following three sentences, inserting quotation marks where appropriate. Remember to press the left Shift key. Press Enter after each line.

1 The computer is old, stated Mr. Barlow, and must be replaced.

2 Why did the pilot say, We'll be 30 minutes late?

3 Catherine sleepily asked, Why don't you just be quiet?

Key the following three sentences of dialog, adding quotation marks as appropriate. Press Tab before each line of dialog and press Enter at the end of each line.

4 We will be landing 30 minutes late, announced the pilot.

5 Deanna muttered, I suppose that means we miss dinner.

6 The flight attendant smiled and said, Perhaps we'll be on time after all.

Key the following paragraph as conversation, adding quotation marks as appropriate. Remember to press Tab at the start of the paragraph. Click the Finished button when you have finished keying the paragraph.

7   The pilot announced, Due to fog, we will be forced to land in Omaha instead of Minneapolis. Deanna's fears were confirmed. Omaha? she blurted. Yes, it's a wonderful city. I vacation there often, replied the flight attendant. The pilot was heard again, We may not be able to leave Omaha for 36 hours. Be prepared to spend the night in the airport. An unexpected treat, said the smiling flight attendant.

**Exercise 19.7** Quotation Marks with Titles and for Emphasis Drill

Key each of the following sentences, inserting quotation marks to enclose titles or special words of emphasis. Press Enter at the end of each line.

1 The story was a real corker.

2 The gemot was used largely in early English government.

3 With friends like you, who needs enemies?

4 A narrow path or ledge is sometimes called a berm.

*drill continues*

7  initiated hesitating alkaline likeness indefinite

8  delegates heightened lengthened stealing gaslight

9  The hesitating delegate is stealing the gaslight.

10  digital lenient distant inkling heading delighted

11  disliked endless athlete install flatten inflated

12  A lenient athlete has inflated the flattened keg.

13  whenever stalwart wholesale handwriting knowledge

14  renovate negotiate imagination tradition rational

15  possible establish observation elaborate ambition

16  Establish rational imagination whenever possible.

17  seashells tasteless steadfast thankless defendant

18  attendant delighted sightless lightness negligent

19  legislate essential stateside skinflint landslide

20  Seashells in the landslide delighted a skinflint.

## Assessing Your Speed and Accuracy

Now that you have practiced the appropriate drills, complete two 1-minute timings using the following paragraph. Note that this is the same text keyed for Timings 13.1 and 13.2.

Each timing will begin as soon as you begin keying. Remember to press Tab at the start of the paragraph. If you finish keying the paragraph before the timing expires, press Enter and start keying the paragraph again.

When time expires, the Online Lab will give you a WPM rate and will highlight any errors you made.

The results of all of your timings will be stored in your Timings Performance report. Compare your rates from Timings 13.3 and 13.4 to your rates from Timings 13.1 and 13.2. Has your speed improved? Did you make fewer errors? If you are not meeting the WPM and error goals identified in the Online Lab, repeat Sessions 11–12.

### 1-Minute Timings

**Timings 13.3–13.4**

    It is good to have honest goals. Nothing is gained if one goes forth in pointless roaming. A major effort is needed to prosper. Isolate those foolish errors and avoid them. Hold to a strong, firm hope and move along.

## Quotation Marks in Written Conversation

Typically when dialog is presented, each new speaker's words are started on a new line (or paragraph) and the text is indented. The quotation marks indicate the beginning and ending of what each individual speaker says. Study these examples:

"The weather is really nasty," said Nancy, "so watch your step out there."
Relaxed, Juanita yawned and said, "Oh, I really hadn't noticed."
"That's because you have been sleeping all morning," murmured Nancy, with a slight sneer in her voice.

## Titles Using Quotation Marks

Quotation marks are used to identify titles of works such as poems; short stories; chapters, essays, and articles in magazines or other larger works; radio and television programs; and short musical works. The following sentences show examples of these uses:

"The Midnight Ride of Paul Revere" is a good poem.
The last episode of "Mad Men" was really interesting.
"Last Rays of Daylight" was a dull short story.
Did the band perform "Stardust" last evening?
I read the article "Thirty Ways to Avoid Work" in the magazine.

## Quotation Marks to Indicate Emphasis

Quotation marks are also used within a sentence to emphasize one or more words. Examples include a technical word used in a nontechnical sentence, slang expressions or terms the reader is unlikely to know, and humorous or sarcastic expressions. (It should be noted that emphasized words are commonly set in italics rather than placed in quotes.) Be careful not to overuse quotation marks in this manner. The following sentences provide a few examples of quotation marks being used for emphasis:

The "Aglaonema" is commonly called the Chinese evergreen.
Nathan loved the concert and thought it was "the bomb."
Their idea of "fast" service is serving one customer at a time.
If the last word of a paragraph appears on a line by itself, the word is an "orphan."

## Quotation Marks with Other Punctuation Symbols

When keying quotation marks with other punctuation symbols, it is important to note the order to present the marks. The following is a list of some of the common rules to remember:

1   Place commas and periods inside the quotation marks. (See the previous examples.)

2   A question mark is placed either inside or outside the ending quotation mark, depending on the sentence logic. Place the question mark inside of the quotation if the quotation is a question.

The owner shouted, "Why don't you just leave?"
She asked, "Do you know if the train is late?"

If the sentence is a question, but the quotation is not, the question mark is set outside of the ending quotation mark, as shown in the following examples.

When did she say, "I shall not return"?
Did he say, "I saw 10 paintings at the exhibit"?

Exclamation points follow the same rule as question marks.

3   When an end quotation is followed by a semicolon or colon, the punctuation symbol follows the end quotation mark.

Last week she announced, "Recreation time will be lengthened"; however, we have not experienced it yet.

I will never forget the first line of "The Tragedy of Macbeth": "When shall we meet again? In thunder, lighting, or rain?"

**Ergonomic Tip**

To minimize eye strain, align the monitor and keyboard directly in front of you.

## Ending the Session

The Online Lab automatically saved the work you completed for this session. You can continue with the next session or exit the Online Lab and continue later.

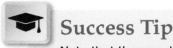

## Success Tip

Note that the apostrophe and the quotation mark are on the same key.

## Correctly Using Apostrophes in Text

The apostrophe has several applications in text. The typical uses of this symbol are listed below.

1  An apostrophe is used in formation of a contraction. A contraction is a word in which one or more letters are omitted. To create a contraction, insert an apostrophe where the letters are omitted.

cannot ──────────→ can't
could not ──────────→ couldn't

Some people have trouble determining if a word is a personal pronoun or a contraction.

their   they're                    its   it's

The apostrophe indicates a missing letter. Therefore, *they're* is a contraction of *they are*, and *it's* stands for *it is*. Some additional examples follow:

They're taking their own sleeping bags.
*not*
They're taking they're (they are) own sleeping bags.

It's a treat to give the dog its bone.
*not*
It's a treat to give the dog it's (it is) bone.

2  When followed by the letter *s*, an apostrophe can show possession.

a hat belonging to John ──→ John's hat
the voices of the people ──→ people's voices
the guess of anybody ──────→ anybody's guess

For plural nouns that end in *s*, add the apostrophe, but do not add an additional *s*.

the carts of the golfers ──────→ golfers' carts
the clothes of the girls ──────→ girls' clothes

3  An apostrophe can be used as a symbol for feet.

100 feet ──────────────→ 100'
255 feet ──────────────→ 255'

**Exercise 19.5**    Complete Exercise 19.5 to practice applying these rules for using apostrophes. Follow the instruction prompts in the Online Lab.

## Correctly Using Quotation Marks in Text

The three most common uses for quotation marks are to indicate spoken words in written materials, to identify titles of specific types of work, and to indicate emphasis.

## Unit 2  Number Row Keys

# Session 19 — Apostrophe, Quotation Mark

## Session Objectives

- **Identify the apostrophe (') and quotation mark (") keys**
- **Practice correct finger positioning for the apostrophe (') and quotation mark (") keys**
- **Apply guidelines for use of the apostrophe and quotation marks**

## Getting Started

**Exercise 19.1**  If you are continuing immediately from Session 18, you may skip the Exercise 19.1 warm-up drill. However, if you exited the Online Lab at the end of Session 18, warm up by completing Exercise 19.1.

## Introducing the Apostrophe and Quotation Keys

**Videos 19.1–19.2**  The apostrophe (') and the quotation mark (") symbols are made by using the same key, and the location of that key is shown in the following diagram. Press the left Shift key when pressing the apostrophe key to type a quotation mark. Watch Videos 19.1 and 19.2 and practice these key reaches.

**Exercises 19.2–19.4**  Complete Exercises 19.2 and 19.3 to learn these new keys. When keying the drill lines, follow the instruction prompts in the Online Lab. Work on improving your general speed and accuracy by completing Exercise 19.4.

**apostrophe, quotation mark**

# Session 14

## 1, 2, 3

### Session Objectives

- **Explore the number row**
- **Identify the 1, 2, and 3 keys**
- **Practice correct finger positioning for the 1, 2, and 3 keys**
- **Read and key numbers as syllables or groups**

## Getting Started

**Exercise 14.1**  If you are continuing immediately from Session 13, you may skip the Exercise 14.1 warm-up drill. However, if you exited the Online Lab at the end of Session 13, warm up by completing Exercise 14.1.

## Introducing the 1, 2, and 3 Keys

This is the first session that provides experience with keying the number row, which is located just above the alphabetic keys on the keyboard. Because numbers and symbols (the percent sign, for example) are used frequently with the alphabetic keys, developing equal skills with numbers, symbols, and letters is important.

Whether you keyboard for personal or business use, you will frequently key numbers. Some of the numbers that occur regularly in textual material include dates, telephone numbers, addresses, ZIP codes, postal zones, age, weights, heights, credit card numbers, and driver's license numbers.

**Videos 14.1–14.3**  The locations of the 1, 2, and 3 keys are shown in the following diagram. Watch Videos 14.1 through 14.3 and practice using these new keys.

**Exercises 14.2–14.5**  Complete Exercises 14.2 through 14.5 to learn these new keys. When keying the drill lines, follow the instruction prompts in the Online Lab.

As you complete these exercises, keep in mind these important guidelines when keying numbers:

- Use the home row method. In other words, anchor the left hand on ASDF and the right hand on JKL;.
- Whenever possible, think of numbers in groups of two or three digits. For example, as you key 11, think *eleven*. As you key 111, think *one eleven*.
- When letters and numbers are combined, think of the letter(s) plus a two- or three-digit number. For example, as you key a111, think *a, one eleven*.

The Online Lab specifies the WPM and error goals. When time expires, the Online Lab will give you a WPM rate and error report for the timing. The results of the timings will be stored in your Timings Performance report.

## 1-Minute Timings

**Timing 18.1**

You can have a friend, representative, or someone else help you. There are groups that can help you find a representative or give you free legal services, if you qualify. There are also representatives who do not charge unless you win your appeal. Your local Social Security office has a list of groups that can help you with your appeal.

**Timing 18.2**

The school will leave the campus, scattered throughout 6.5 acres in the area's academic and commercial center, for a new 23-story facility in Salem. The proposal includes open space, saving of many existing buildings, housing for varying income levels, and parking for the community. The cost is expected to be $1 billion.

The following 3-minute timing will help prepare you for keying longer documents, such as reports. Speed generally decreases and errors generally increase when the duration of the timing is extended.

## 3-Minute Timing

**Timing 18.3**

Nails date back to 3000 BCE. They have been found in diggings and sunken ships that sailed in the years around 500 CE. The Romans hand-forged nails and began the new trend toward routine use in building with wood. Most nails were first made in small shops; demand for nails grew so fast that the small but well-made supply of handmade nails was not quite enough for the demand. Today, most companies that make nails can trace their own beginnings back to those early times.

 **Ergonomic Tip**

If you don't have a document stand handy, be creative. Use a clothespin or magnets to hold your source material (but don't attach magnets to computers, monitors, or other electronics). Remember to position the source text the same distance from your eyes as the screen.

## Ending the Session

The Online Lab automatically saved the work you completed for this session. You can continue with the next session or exit the Online Lab and continue later.

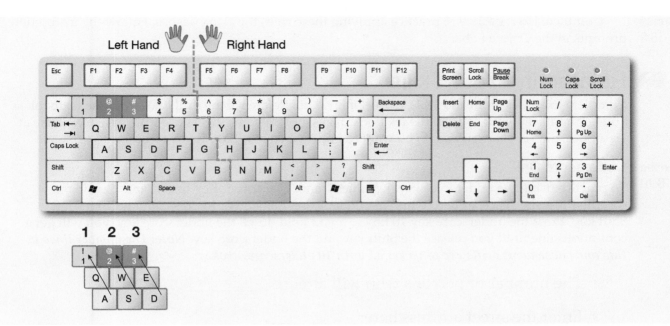

## Reinforcing Your Skills

Complete Exercises 14.6 through 14.12 in the Online Lab. Reference the drill lines from the textbook as you key and keep your eyes on the textbook pages, not on your fingers. Complete each exercise at least once, but repeat exercises if you want to improve your WPM rate or accuracy.

**Exercise 14.6**

**1 Drill**

Key line 1 once for speed. Your WPM rate will appear after keying the line.

Key line 2 once for control. Try to reach 25 WPM and make two or fewer errors (or follow the goals set by your instructor). Your WPM rate will appear after keying the line, and any errors will be highlighted.

1  a1 1a1 a111 a1 a1 a11 a111 a1 11a11 a1 1a1 a11 a1

2  a11 a111 11a a1 1a1 a11 111a 111 11a 11 a1 11a 1a

**Exercise 14.7**

**2 Drill**

Key line 1 once for speed. Your WPM rate will appear after keying the line.

Key line 2 once for control. Try to reach 25 WPM and make two or fewer errors (or follow the goals set by your instructor). Your WPM rate will appear after keying the line, and any errors will be highlighted.

1  1 2 1 21 221 122 121 221 2 1 212 112 1 12 21 21 2

2  a12 2a1 112a 12a12 21a1 122a a11 a2a 12a 1a2a 122

**Success Tip**

When keying the number 21, think *twenty-one*, not *two one*. When keying 221, think *two, twenty-one*. When keying 112a, think *one, twelve-a*.

**Exercise 18.9**     Complete Exercise 18.9 to practice applying these rules for using dashes. Follow the instruction prompts in the Online Lab.

## ➤➤ Reinforcing Your Skills

Complete Exercises 18.10 and 18.11 in the Online Lab. Reference the drill lines from the textbook as you key and keep your eyes on the textbook pages, not on your fingers. Complete each exercise at least once, but repeat exercises if you want to improve your WPM rate or accuracy.

**Exercise 18.10**    Underscore Drill

To practice using the underscore key, key lines 1 and 2 for speed. Key lines 1 and 2 again for control. Press the spacebar before the first underscore. Remember to press (and hold) the left Shift key. Press the underscore key 10 times. If you hold down the underscore key, you will get a continuous line until you release the Shift key and the underscore key. *Note: The answer lines in this and subsequent drills are to be keyed with 10 underscore strokes.*

1 The number of persons who will attend: _____.

2 Enter the street address here: _____.

**Exercise 18.11**    Reinforcement Drill

Key the following lines once. Press Enter after each line.

1 ;-; ;-; ;-; ;-; ;-; ;- ;- -;-; ;-; ;-; ;- ;- ;-

2 ex-roommate, self-taught, cross-country, one and one-third

3 sixty-six, a self-employed person, a last-minute effort

4 one hundred fifty-six, eight-cylinder engine, twenty-six

5 ;--; ;--; --;--; --;--; ;--; -- -- ;--; --;--; --

6 There is a flaw in the plan--a fatal one.

7 All books--fiction, poetry, and drama--are on sale.

8 I said once--and I will say it again--I disagree.

9 I cooked the meal--but they got the credit for it.

10 ;-;_ ;- _;_ _;_ -- -- ;_;_ ;-_; ;-_; __ ;- ;_;_;_ ;-;_

11 The pin number is _____.

12 Enter your name here: _____

## Assessing Your Speed and Accuracy

Complete Timings 18.1 through 18.3 in the Online Lab. Refer to the following paragraphs from the textbook as you key.

Each timing will start as soon as you begin keying. Remember to press Tab at the start of the paragraph. If you finish keying the paragraph before time expires, press Enter and start keying the paragraph again.

**Exercise 14.8** Numbers with Four Digits Drill

When working with groups of numbers having four digits and no natural break, think of the numbers as two pairs. For example, the number 1221 is read as *twelve, twenty-one.*

Key lines 1 and 2 once for speed. Read the numbers in pairs to gain speed while keying.

1  1221 1112 1221 1112 2112 2112 1122 1122 1221 2221

2  a1122 a1221 1112a 1212a a1112 a2112 a1212 a1221a2

**Exercise 14.9** Numbers with Five or More Digits Drill

Use a two-three-two reading pattern when keying number groups with more than four digits and no natural breaks such as spaces, commas, or decimals. For example, read the number 2121221 as *twenty-one, two-twelve, twenty-one.* For the number 21221, think *twenty-one, two twenty-one* (two-three reading pattern).

Key lines 1–5 once. Mentally pronounce the number combinations as you key them. Try to reach 25 WPM and make two or fewer errors (or follow the goals set by your instructor). Your WPM rate will appear after keying each line, and any errors will be highlighted.

1  21 221 21 221 21 221 a21 212a 12 11a 2121 a121 a2

2  21221 21121 21221 a21112 a12212 a12121 21212 a122

3  a2112121 22 1 21a 2122121 12221 a212a 1221a 12221

4  12 12 12 12 121 121 121 121 a2a a221 a221 2a211 1

5  212a1 121221a 12122a1 22221a 12212a 221221a 21a22

 **Success Tip**

Keep your fingers on the home row and reach from that position to key a particular number or several numbers. Return your finger to the home row position after keying the number or numbers.

**Exercise 14.10** 3 Drill

Key lines 1 and 2 once for speed. Your WPM rate will appear after keying each line.

Key line 3 once for control. Try to reach 25 WPM and make two or fewer errors (or follow the goals set by your instructor). Your WPM rate will appear after keying the line, and any errors will be highlighted.

1  332 32 213 231 12 1321 231 32 231 2312 232 1213 3

2  a33 a3 a32 a321 a233 a3232 a132 13232 3223212 a23

3  a323 a3212321 a13231a a1 231a a123 232 32 332 a13

**Exercises**
**18.5–18.6**   Complete Exercises 18.5 and 18.6 to practice applying these word division rules. Follow the instruction prompts in the Online Lab.

## General Guidelines for Compound Words and Numbers

The following guidelines will explain when to use hyphens in compound words, such as compound adjectives and the words in spelled-out fractions. Do not press the spacebar before or after the hyphen key.

1   Use a hyphen to combine compound adjectives that describe a noun.

> a 15-story building
>
> the still-active volcano
>
> a slow-moving snail

2   If the word combination is used as a unit after a noun, do not use a hyphen.

> a building 15 stories high
>
> the volcano that is still active
>
> a snail that is slow moving

3   Do not use a hyphen when the first word in a compound adjective is an adverb ending in ly.

> a highly rated movie
>
> a quickly moving car

4   Compound words beginning with *ex* and *self* are usually hyphenated.

> ex-roommate
>
> self-taught

5   In nontechnical text, hyphenate spelled-out fractions and spelled-out numbers between 21 and 99, if they stand alone or if they are used with numbers beyond 100. Do not hyphenate numerals.

> one and one-third miles
>
> seventy-six trombones
>
> one hundred sixty-six people

**Exercises**
**18.7–18.8**   Complete Exercises 18.7 and 18.8 to practice applying these guidelines for using hyphens in compound words and numbers. Follow the instruction prompts in the Online Lab.

## Correctly Using Dashes in Text

A dash is also called an *em dash* because its length is roughly equivalent to the length of the capital *M* in a given font. Create a dash symbol by typing two hyphens. Typically word processing programs will automatically replace two hyphens with a dash when a space is keyed after a word following the two hyphens. Do not press the spacebar before, between, or after the double hyphens. Do not key a space before or after a dash.

The dash is commonly used in one of four instances.

1   In place of quotation marks to set off dialog.

2   To avoid the confusion of too many commas in a sentence.

> All books—fiction, poetry, and drama—are on sale.

3   For special emphasis.

> I cooked the meal—but they got the credit for it.
>
> There is a flaw in the plan—a fatal one.

4   To indicate a side comment, instead of using parenthesis.

> I said once—when we were in the garden—I disagree.

**Exercise 14.11**

Sentences Drill

Key each drill line twice and push for speed. Try to reach 25 WPM (or the goal set by your instructor). Your WPM rate will appear after keying each line.

1 Jean shall sell the 321 seashells and 212 stones.
2 Taste the lean tea; handle the kettle that leaks.
3 The 11 attendants halted a ring of thieves. They felt proud.

Key lines 4–6 once and then key the three lines again. Concentrate on control. Try to reach 25 WPM and make two or fewer errors (or follow the goals set by your instructor). Your WPM rate will appear after keying the line, and any errors will be highlighted.

4 See, he is ill; his skin is flushed; he feels faint.
5 Enlist the 13 students to help with the many tasks.
6 She is a skilled athlete who strives for perfection.

 **Success Tip**

Reading numbers in groups will help you gain speed and improve accuracy. This method is also known as *syllabizing* numbers.

**Exercise 14.12**

Reinforcement Drill

As you key the following drill, remember to mentally read numbers with two or more digits in groups.

Key lines 1 and 2 once for speed. Your WPM rate will appear after keying each line.

1 2 21 21 12 1 112 212 1 2 221 121 121 221 21 1 2 1
2 222 222 22 222 2 222 222 22 2 2 222 222 22 22 2 2

Key line 3 once for control. Try to reach 25 WPM and make two or fewer errors (or follow the goals set by your instructor). Your WPM rate will appear after keying the line, and any errors will be highlighted.

3 3 3 3 33 33 33 33 33 333 33 33 3 3 3 33 33 33 3 3 3

Follow the previous drill instructions and key lines 4 and 5 once for speed. Key line 6 once for control.

4 1231 3323 321 13 33212 323321 233 23 231 13 233 3
5 a22132213 a21321 2331 2a 22312a 231132a 323132112
6 3112 1232 3321 2311 3122 1312 3222 3221 1223 1233

*drill continues*

# Correctly Using Hyphens in Text

The hyphen is a versatile punctuation mark that has several applications. The hyphen indicates where a word is divided across a line break. The hyphen also connects words, such as compound adjectives and the words in spelled-out fractions. Finally, a hyphen can be used to indicate subtraction, as in 100 - 25 = 75.

## General Guidelines for Word Division

As noted previously, most word processing programs use word wrap, so the keyboardist does not need to define each line break by pressing the Enter key. Instead, Enter is pressed only at the end of a paragraph. When using word wrap, typically the software will start a new line with the start of a new word, but word processing programs also allow words to hyphenate, or *break*, at the end of lines. Although hyphenating words can make them more difficult to read, hyphenation can allow a page of text to have a more visually consistent right margin (the blank part of the page to the right of the text). Most word processing programs offer an automatic hyphenation feature, and some software asks the user to make hyphenation decisions during the hyphenating process.

The following guidelines include the essential rules for determining where to break words, but note that some of these rules have exceptions. If in doubt, consult a dictionary for the appropriate place to break a particular word.

1   Leave three or more letters of a word at the end of a line and carry over three or more letters to the next line. This rule is commonly modified, since some software programs leave or carry over only two letters of a word when automatic hyphenation is used.

2   Do not divide the last word of a paragraph or a page.

3   Do not key more than two consecutive lines that end with hyphens. This rule is commonly modified to allow three lines with automatic hyphenation.

4   Divide words using the following rules:

| Rule | Example | Correct Division |
|---|---|---|
| between syllables according to pronunciation | provoke | pro-voke |
| between two consonants unless a root word would be destroyed | napkin<br>billing | nap-kin<br>bill-ing (not bil-ling) |
| between two vowels that are pronounced separately | continuation | continu-ation |
| after a one-syllable vowel | benefactor | bene-factor |
| between two parts of a compound word | salesperson | sales-person |

5   The following are examples of words or phrases that should *not* be divided:

| Word or Phrase Type | Example | Incorrect Division |
|---|---|---|
| words of one syllable | storm | sto-rm |
| words with a one-letter prefix | along<br>enough | a-long<br>e-nough |
| syllable with a silent vowel sound | yelled<br>strained | yel-led<br>strain-ed |
| proper nouns, abbreviations, contractions, or number combinations | Barbara<br>FBI<br>couldn't<br>31 Oak Lane<br>March 14 | Bar-bara<br>F-BI<br>could-n't<br>3-1 Oak Lane<br>March 1-4 |

Follow the previous drill instructions and key lines 7 and 8 once for speed. Key line 9 once for control.

⁊ 23 3231 2231 123 121 233 32 12131 221312 31131 12

⁸ 3123 123212 133132 123 321233 3112 32 132 1132 21

⁹ 32 321 33312 12 3 23222123 1122331 12 1223 311132

## Assessing Your Speed and Accuracy

Complete Timings 14.1 and 14.2 in the Online Lab to assess the skills you have learned. Refer to the following paragraphs as you key. *Note: With this session, the default WPM goal for 1-minute timings has been increased by 5 WPM in the Online Lab. However, your instructor may have customized this goal.*

Each timing will start as soon as you begin keying. Remember to press Tab at the start of the paragraph. If you finish keying the paragraph before the timing expires, press Enter and start keying the paragraph again.

The Online Lab specifies the WPM and error goals. When time expires, the Online Lab will give you a WPM rate and will highlight any errors you made. The results will be stored in your Timings Performance report.

### 1-Minute Timings

**Timing 14.1**
When business is weak, there is not a lot of demand for money. So savings are invested in the stock market. The prices of stocks and bonds go up and interest rates go down. When business is strong, the demand for loans goes up to expand production, and consumers buy cars and homes. This pushes interest rates up.

**Timing 14.2**
The blunt auditor suggested to Duke that the business returns were a fraud. The usual routine of minimum turnovers of funds had been sound, but that fortune of thousands paid to the 12 jurors had not been inserted in the annual input. Duke presumed he was ruined and flushed with guilt.

 **Ergonomic Tip**

Sit in a slightly reclined position with your thighs parallel to each other. In other words, do not cross your legs, as it decreases circulation.

## Ending the Session

The Online Lab automatically saved the work you completed for this session. You can continue with the next session or exit the Online Lab and continue later.

# Session 18

# Hyphen, Underscore

## Session Objectives

- Identify the hyphen (-) and underscore (_) keys
- Practice correct finger positioning for the hyphen (-) and underscore (_) keys
- Explore hyphenating words and using dashes
- Utilize rules for division of words and compound words

## Getting Started

**Exercise 18.1** If you are continuing immediately from Session 17, you may skip the Exercise 18.1 warm-up drill. However, if you exited the Online Lab at the end of Session 17, warm up by completing Exercise 18.1.

## Introducing the Hyphen and Underscore Keys

**Videos 18.1–18.2** The hyphen (-) and underscore (_) symbols are made by using the same key, and the location of that key is shown in the following diagram. Strike the hyphen key twice to key a dash (--). Press the left Shift key when pressing the hyphen key to type an underscore. The underscore symbol is also called the *underline symbol*. Watch Videos 18.1 and 18.2 and practice these key reaches.

**Exercises 18.2–18.4** Complete Exercises 18.2 and 18.3 to learn these new keys. When keying the drill lines, follow the instruction prompts in the Online Lab. Work on improving your general speed and accuracy by completing Exercise 18.4.

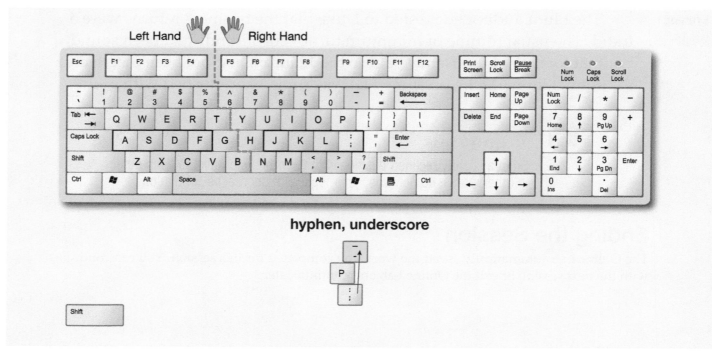

hyphen, underscore

# Session
## 15
# 4, 5, 6

## Session Objectives

- **Identify the 4, 5, and 6 keys**
- **Practice correct finger positioning for the 4, 5, and 6 keys**

## Getting Started

**Exercise 15.1** If you are continuing immediately from Session 14, you may skip the Exercise 15.1 warm-up drill. However, if you exited the Online Lab at the end of Session 14, warm up by completing Exercise 15.1.

## Introducing the 4, 5, and 6 Keys

**Videos 15.1–15.3** The locations of the 4, 5, and 6 keys are shown in the following diagram. Watch Videos 15.1 through 15.3 and practice using these new keys.

**Exercises 15.2–15.7** Complete Exercises 15.2 through 15.7 to learn these new keys. When keying the drill lines, follow the instruction prompts in the Online Lab.

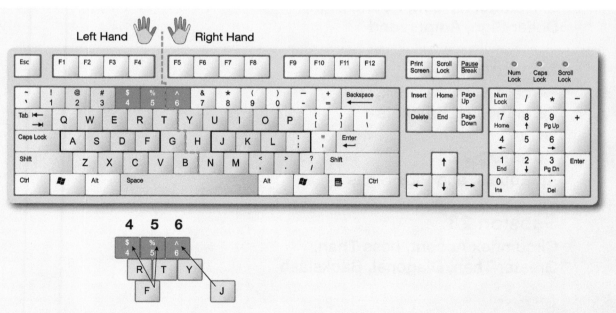

## Reinforcing Your Skills

Complete Exercises 15.8 through 15.12 in the Online Lab. Reference the drill lines from the textbook as you key and keep your eyes on the textbook pages, not on your fingers. Complete each exercise at least once, but repeat exercises if you want to improve your WPM rate or accuracy.

**Exercise 4 Drill**
**15.8**

Key lines 1 and 2 once for speed. You will key faster if you think of the numbers in groups. Try to reach 25 WPM (or the goal set by your instructor). Your WPM rate will appear after keying each line.

1 14 134 1431 2343 343123 43 334 3 3421 23214 432442

2 a14 a4231 24 4a24 1432a 34 a4321 a4323 a431 a342 a

Key line 3 once and concentrate on control. Try to reach 25 WPM and make two or fewer errors (or follow the goals set by your instructor). Your WPM rate will appear after keying the line, and any errors will be highlighted.

3 4343213413 34343213311 4323412341 3431233 44342 43

**Exercise 5 Drill**
**15.9**

Key lines 1 and 2 once for speed. Try to reach 25 WPM (or the goal set by your instructor). Your WPM rate will appear after keying each line.

1 11 55 a55 11 55 a55 11 55 55 11 51 a51 15 15 15 5

2 55 44 a45 54 14 15 24 25 34 35 53 43 52 42 51 41a

Key line 3 once and concentrate on control. Try to reach 25 WPM and make two or fewer errors (or follow the goals set by your instructor). Your WPM rate will appear after keying the line, and any errors will be highlighted.

3 15115 15115 a55151 a55151 15 5151 151 a155 a51151

**Exercise 6 Drill**
**15.10**

Key lines 1 and 2 once for speed. Try to reach 25 WPM (or the goal set by your instructor). Your WPM rate will appear after keying each line.

1 11 a66 11 66 11 66 11 66 11 66 a66 11 66 11 66 61

2 166 166 a661 661 161 161 a611 661 661 116 11 a666

Key line 3 once and concentrate on control. Try to reach 25 WPM and make two or fewer errors (or follow the goals set by your instructor). Your WPM rate will appear after keying the line, and any errors will be highlighted.

3 11666 16661 61 66 66 111 666 661 1166 16661 61 61

**Ergonomic Tip**

You should not have to reach for your keyboard. Move the keyboard so that you can keep your elbows at your side as you position your fingers over the home row keys.

## Ending the Session

The Online Lab automatically saved the work you completed for this session. You can continue with the next session or exit the Online Lab and continue later.

**Success Tip**

Do not touch the key between the home row and the number key you are entering; this would slow you down. In addition, note that all keyboards do not have the same alignment.

**Exercise 15.11** Reinforcement Drill

Key lines 1 and 2 once for speed. Try to reach 25 WPM (or the goal set by your instructor). Your WPM rate will appear after keying each line.

1  44 44 444 44 44 44 4 4444 44 4 4 444 444 44 44 4 4

2  334 44 343 22343 3443 23423 3422 4321 343 344 43 4

Key line 3 once and concentrate on control. Try to reach 25 WPM and make two or fewer errors (or follow the goals set by your instructor). Your WPM rate will appear after keying the line, and any errors will be highlighted.

3  43 44342 3431233 4323412341 34343213311 4343213413

Follow the previous speed instructions for lines 4–5 and 7–8. Follow the previous control instructions for lines 6 and 9.

4  151 51 55 51 55 15 51 15 15 15 5 5 5 55 55 55 5 5

5  51 15115 155 151 51511 15 55151 55151 15115 15115

6  123 a15a a15a a321 a321a21515 a21515 15115 15115

7  6 61 61 61 61 61 666 666 6 6 6 6 66 66 66 66 6 6 6

8  a666 111 116 661 661 a611 161 161 661 a661 166 166

9  61 61 16661 1166 661 666 111 66 66 61 16661 11666

## Assessing Your Speed and Accuracy

Complete Timings 17.1 through 17.4 in the Online Lab. Timing 17.1 will assess your number keying skills learned in Sessions 14–17, whereas Timings 17.2 through 17.4 will assess your general keying skills. Refer to the following numerical text or paragraphs as you key. The timings will start as soon as you begin keying. For each timing, if you complete keying all lines before time expires, press Enter and start keying the first line again.

The Online Lab specifies WPM and error goals. When time expires, the Online Lab will give you a WPM rate and will highlight any errors you made. The results will be stored in your Timings Performance report.

*Hint: For the number timing, Timing 17.1, press Enter at the end of each line.*

### 1-Minute Timing

**Timing 17.1**

10 10 5,854 22.30 853375 55102 4,209.55 76,238,974 500.54
55,000 212,887 79,237 99,723.54 2,200 7978 33,344 897 2366
1133 477 98,545 28544 90,255.54 850 198,355 67,284 334542
1p14 2013 3030 2019 71523 36274 18054 55,112,445 459,100
1 4 8 0 38 87 61 90 47k2 874 982 380 5843 8787 45,88,10,21,34

For Timings 17.2 through 17.4 refer to the following paragraphs as you key. Remember to press Tab at the beginning of a paragraph.

### 1-Minute Timings

**Timing 17.2**

The United States Agency for International Development sponsors a speakers program that provides citizens with an opportunity to learn about the culture of other countries. Educators, business men and women, and school administrators with a need to have firsthand information are eligible. More than 125 countries participate in this program.

**Timing 17.3**

A career in science involves selecting a path among several options. One could choose to become a doctor in a clinic or a teacher in a medical school. An active search through more than 190 college catalogs will indicate which courses to select. Contact campus finance officers to check cost factors.

**Timing 17.4**

Mack, a black Scottie, is a champion canine. A constant companion is the yellow cat called Chicco. Crowds laugh and applaud as Mack and Chicco do their tricks to music. Mack can count 15 objects and walk on his hind legs. Chicco jumps over Mack, adding a certain clownish touch to the act.

**Exercise
15.12**

Sentences Drill

Key lines 1–10 once for speed. Try to reach 30 WPM (or the goal set by your instructor). Your WPM rate will appear after keying each line.

Key lines 1–10 again. This time, focus on control. Try to reach 30 WPM and make two or fewer errors (or follow the goals set by your instructor). Your WPM rate will appear after keying each line, and any errors will be highlighted.

1 Dennis and Gene nailed 16 boards onto the old gate.

2 Helen had seen the 12 lighted signs shining at night.

3 Anne and Bill ate a salad and 15 figs and a big steak.

4 Leslie sang a tiny jingle as she dashed ahead in glee.

5 When Tom tested his stiff ankle, he gnashed his teeth.

6 Please appease that helpless, pleading, pious plaintiff.

7 A tall, split, peeling aspen sapling is plainly diseased.

8 Pat speaks and pleads and defends the 14 plaintiffs.

9 Did Tim tape that splint and dispense the correct pills?

10 The spaniel has 134 bites and needs some skilled help.

## Assessing Your Speed and Accuracy

Complete Timings 15.1 through 15.5 in the Online Lab to assess the skills you have learned in this session. Timings 15.1 and 15.2 are timings on lines of numbers and Timings 15.3 through 15.5 are text-based paragraphs that include numbers. Refer to the following timing text as you key.

Each timing will start as soon as you begin keying. If you finish keying before the timing expires, press Enter and start keying the timing text again.

The Online Lab specifies the WPM and error goals. When time expires, the Online Lab will give you a WPM rate and will highlight any errors you made. The results will be stored in your Timings Performance report.

*Hint: For the number timings, Timings 15.1 and 15.2, press Enter at the end of each line.*

1-Minute Timings

**Timing
15.1**

333 333 333 444 444 444 555 555 555 666 666 666 56
333 333 444 444 555 666 666 111 111 222 222 123 45
12223 12224 13335 13336 14442 14443 12224 12225 16
32221 42221 53331 63331 24441 34441 42221 52221 63

**Timing
15.2**

26 35 346 34 45 46 251 2346 235 325 625 463 51616 2
6242 4621 31446 51432 51431 4265 4261 5431 5421 6
16 61 61 31 31 31 3655 66 16 62 5661 6546 665 566 2
16 661 626 365 4466 1263 4565 16 15 1615 26 62 54 3

**9** For ages, follow the general guidelines for numbers.

  15 He is 20 years old.

  16 She is nine months old.

**10** Use numerals to express clock time.

  17 Pack your bags right away so we can make the 5:20 p.m. flight.

**11** Key house numbers in numerals.

  18 His address is 13038 N. Westgate Drive.

**12** Spell out street names that contain numbers below 10. If the numbers are 10 or above, express the names in numerals.

  19 The store is located on First Avenue.

  20 My address is 17815 N. 13th Avenue.

**Exercise 17.13**  Sentences Drill

Key lines 1–10 once for speed. Try to reach 25 WPM (or the goal set by your instructor). Your WPM rate will appear at the end of each line.

Key lines 1–10 again. This time, focus on control. Try to reach 30 WPM and make two or fewer errors (or follow the goals set by your instructor). Your WPM rate will appear at the end of each line, and any errors will be highlighted.

  1 Did Van ever deliver the varnish and the 150 shelves?

  2 Vinnie lives in their villa; he enjoys the vast veranda.

  3 It is evident; the vital lever reverses the vexing vent.

  4 Ron delivered the 18 leather chairs late this evening.

  5 Marvel served 286 vanilla shakes at 2 gala events.

  6 The driver developed a fever; give him two vitamins.

  7 That starving animal evaded 103 vigilant observers.

  8 She does not fool them; she is not an honest senator.

  9 Opal ordered 4 onions and 79 olives from the market.

  10 Did the florist remove all the thorns from the roses?

Complete 1-minute timings on each of the paragraphs below. Remember to press Tab at the start of each paragraph.

1-Minute Timings

**Timing**
**15.3**

During the winter, the jet stream migrates north. For the northern Midwest, this is observed as cold and dry air. It is not unusual for temperatures to plunge well below zero. Any precipitation is usually in the form of snow. Because the air is dry, snowfall amounts are generally not large. However, when weather fronts travel from the south, the collision of these moist systems with cold northern air can produce very large snowfalls of 10 or 20 inches.

**Timing**
**15.4**

Muffin is a genuine bulldog. Although he weighs 64 pounds, he bounds about with a flourish. It is fun to see him plunge around, indulging in the pure pleasure of running. He huffs and puffs and slumps to the ground. No doubt he will jump and lunge again, after a pause, and find trouble.

**Timing**
**15.5**

Thomas bought a used car from a dealer at 16532 Halsted Street. Although the bumper and the trunk were ruined, he assumed that it would run. If he would flush the rust from the lumbering hulk of junk, he might be able to use it. His woeful anguish spurred a new thought; perhaps it was useless.

 Ergonomic Tip
Keep both feet flat on the floor or on a footrest to minimize fatigue.

## Ending the Session

The Online Lab automatically saved the work you completed for this session. You can continue with the next session or exit the Online Lab and continue later.

**Exercise 17.12**

**Guidelines for Expressing Numbers Drill**

Organizations do not always agree on when to spell out numbers and when to use numerals. However, the following guidelines are widely accepted. For each guideline, key the examples in the Online Lab, pressing Enter after each line. To help you impress a mental image of the examples for each guideline, reread what you have keyed after keying each line.

1  Spell out numbers zero through nine. Use numerals for multiple-digit numbers, 10 and above.

   1  The computer science class includes six women.

   2  At least 40 men are enrolled in beginning keyboarding.

2  If any of the numbers in a series or sentence is made up of two or more digits (numbers 10 and above), use numerals for all the numbers, including the single-digit numbers.

   3  We have 16 Compaq computers, 14 Dell computers, and 8 Gateway computers.

3  When a sentence begins with a number, spell it out (or rewrite the sentence).

   4  Three hundred students are majoring in business.

   5  Business majors number 300.

4  If the day of the month precedes the month, express it in words.

   6  We will meet on the sixth of December.

5  If the day of the month follows the month, express it in numerals.

   7  We will meet on December 6 at the restaurant.

6  If the date is in the form of month, day, and year, express the day and year in numerals. Always follow the day and year with commas, unless the year appears at the end of a sentence.

   8  We will meet on December 6, 2014, at the restaurant.

7  Use numerals for measurements, percentages, and other mathematical expressions.

   9  We need new carpet for a room that is 11 feet x 12 feet.

   10  The package weighs about 7 pounds.

   11  I will ask for a 6 percent raise.

8  In general, use numerals to express fractions and mixed numbers of physical measurements or in technical writing. If a fraction appears alone—does not express a direct physical measurement—spell out the fraction.

   12  They used 3.5 feet of coaxial cable.

   13  He makes only half of what she makes.

   14  He is 6.5 feet tall.

*drill continues*

# Session 16

# 7, 8, 9, 0, Comma, Decimal Point

## Session Objectives

- **Identify the 7, 8, 9, and 0 keys**
- **Practice correct finger positioning for the 7, 8, 9, and 0 keys**
- **Explore using the comma and decimal keys**

## Getting Started

**Exercise 16.1** If you are continuing immediately from Session 15, you may skip the Exercise 16.1 warm-up drill. However, if you exited the Online Lab at the end of Session 15, warm up by completing Exercise 16.1.

## Introducing the 7, 8, 9, and 0 Keys

**Videos 16.1–16.4** The locations of the 7, 8, 9, and 0 keys are shown in the following diagram. Watch Videos 16.1 through 16.4 and practice using these new keys.

**Exercises 16.2–16.6** Complete Exercises 16.2 through 16.6 to learn these new keys. When keying the drill lines, follow the instruction prompts in the Online Lab.

### Success Tip

To create groups of numbers in columns, use the tab feature to move across the columns. It is more efficient to tab across columns instead of keying all the numbers in all rows of a single column before moving to the next column.

**Exercise 17.10** Numbers Drill

Key lines 1 and 2 once for speed. Remember to read the numbers in two-three-two combinations. Try to reach 25 WPM (or the goal set by your instructor). Your WPM rate will appear after keying each line.

1 7371130 91368840 1534986003 51673455189 963310931

2 21468159 515113 6873931 438761 223026501 89340013

Key line 3 once and concentrate on control. Try to key without error (or follow the goal set by your instructor). Your WPM rate will appear after keying each line, and any errors will be highlighted.

3 6135910 619822385 3676 1090101 3948131 1788434341

**Exercise 17.11** Reinforcement Drill

Key lines 1 and 2 once for speed. Remember to read the numbers in two-three-two combinations. Try to reach 25 WPM (or the goal set by your instructor). Your WPM rate will appear after keying each line.

1 2 34141 38886190 1 5133459 789 386005138 45134157

2 9,586,713 39,913,867 55,565,577 231,464 2,361,731

Key line 3 once and concentrate on control. Try to key without error (or follow the goal set by your instructor). Your WPM rate will appear after keying each line, and any errors will be highlighted.

3 4,131 59.39 13,667 63,485 .98 78,431 40.83 76,924

Follow the previous *speed* instructions for lines 4–5 and 7–8. Follow the previous *control* instructions for lines 6 and 9.

4 47 681107 741 23 15281 59,602,388 2.95 96175 284 4

5 56451089 904 82 67,832,523.15 571.28 903 84.22 99

6 15 510 67414451 281,401,282.00 61700 29.15 106 80

7 4559 71.26 8674005 21 4.86 489,753 4605141 50 224

8 531 78911 556 9,454.89 49724301 5,410 8.26 667101

9 2,466 61780 434215 5436 33216 4457004 96.48 82 46

## ➤➤ Reinforcing Your Skills

Complete Exercises 16.7 through 16.16 in the Online Lab. Reference the drill lines from the textbook as you key and keep your eyes on the textbook pages, not on your fingers. Complete each exercise at least once, but repeat exercises if you want to improve your WPM rate or accuracy.

**Exercise** **7 Drill**
**16.7**

Key lines 1 and 2 once for speed. Anchor the ; (semicolon) finger on the home row. Try to reach 25 WPM (or the goal set by your instructor). Your WPM rate will appear after keying each line.

1  a55 77 66 76 57 57 a76 77 777 677 a555 76 6 a755a a755a

2  767 767 5767 5757 a576 7675a 7675a 77 777 666 555 a75a

Key line 3 once and concentrate on control. Try to reach 25 WPM and make two or fewer errors (or follow the goals set by your instructor). Your WPM rate will appear after keying each line, and any errors will be highlighted.

3  a576a 76a5a 6675a 6675 5667 777 a65a7 5672 a7765 a575a

**Exercise** **1–7 Drill**
**16.8**

To develop speed keying the numbers 1–7, see how quickly you can complete the following:

1  Key the numbers 1 through 7 three times. Space once between numbers and press Enter at the end of each number set. Keep your eyes on the screen.

2  Reverse the order and key the numbers 7 down through 1 three times. Space once between numbers and press Enter at the end of each number set. Again, keep your eyes on the screen.

 **Success Tip**

After keying the numbers 7 down to 1, proofread. If you have any errors, repeat the drill until you can key the numbers without error.

**Exercise** **8 Drill**
**16.9**

Key lines 1 and 2 once for speed. Anchor either the J or the ; (semicolon) finger on the home row when keying 8. Try to reach 25 WPM (or the goal set by your instructor). Your WPM rate will appear after keying each line.

1  88 11 588 11 88 11 88 11 88 11 688 11 88 11 8 8823 1482

2  8182 81828 2845 6817 71882 6818 2238 885 888 288 388

Key line 3 once and concentrate control. Try to reach 25 WPM and make two or fewer errors (or follow the goals set by your instructor). After keying, your WPM rate and any errors will display.

3  557 8283 38482 78681 11812 8823 28 28 888 321 854 488

**Exercise** **1–8 Drill**
**16.10**

Complete the following drill to develop speed and concentration.

1  Key the numbers 1 through 8 three times. Space once between numbers and press Enter at the end of each number set. Keep your eyes on the screen.

2  Reverse the order and key the numbers 8 down through 1 three times. Space once between numbers and press Enter at the end of each number set. Again, keep your eyes on the screen.

**Exercise 17.6** Most Common Digits Drill

The most frequently used digit is 0, followed by 5. To build your skills with these digits, key to 500 by tens, and then key to 200 by fives. Space once between numbers. Press Enter after keying the final number; your WPM rate will appear and any errors will be highlighted. Concentrate on keying without error while maintaining your WPM rate.

1  10 20 30 40 50 60 …

2  5 10 15 20 25 30 35 40 45 50 …

**Exercise 17.7** Numbers by Threes Drill

To reinforce your ability to think while keying numbers, start at 100 and key to 1 by threes.

1  100 97 94 91 88 85 82 79 …

Repeat drills 17.5–17.7 as often as you can. They will help you key numbers accurately.

**Exercise 17.8** Reading Number Groups Drill

As a reminder, when a number is segmented naturally by commas, spaces, and decimals, read the number by those groups. For example, read 1,676,352.17 as *one, comma, six seventy-six, comma, three fifty-two, decimal, seventeen*.

Key lines 1 and 2 once for speed. Concentrate on reading numbers in groups. Try to reach 25 WPM (or the goal set by your instructor). Your WPM rate will appear at the end of each line.

1  1,676,352.17 3,131 2.24 436,342 101.31 166,891 89

2  236,731 831,643 534.67 4,091,867 3,587.13 501,316

Key line 3 once and concentrate on control. Try to key without error (or follow the goal set by your instructor). Your WPM rate will appear after keying each line, and any errors will be highlighted.

3  61,301.04 .36 89,341.76 31,700.73 151,317 416,319

**Exercise 17.9** Columns of Numbers Drill

Using the tabs preset at every 0.5 inch, create the following columns of numbers by keying the first four-digit number and then pressing the Tab key to move to the next columns. Press Enter at the end of each line.

Key the columns of numbers for control. Try to key without error (or follow the goal set by your instructor). Your WPM rate will appear after keying each line, and any errors will be highlighted.

| | | | | |
|---|---|---|---|---|
| 1  4901 | 8702 | 3303 | 3904 | 7205 |
| 2  6106 | 8307 | 9408 | 2709 | 3710 |
| 3  1511 | 5712 | 2613 | 9114 | 1515 |
| 4  5716 | 9117 | 5618 | 6619 | 3820 |
| 5  2621 | 3122 | 4523 | 2324 | 3125 |
| 6  6726 | 3528 | 8528 | 3529 | 4130 |
| 7  7731 | 6932 | 8533 | 7434 | 9935 |
| 8  8836 | 2337 | 6138 | 1639 | 5840 |

**Exercise 16.11**    **9 Drill**

Key lines 1 and 2 once for speed. Anchor the J finger on the home row as the L finger keys 9. Remember to read the numbers as groups. Try to reach 25 WPM (or the goal set by your instructor). Your WPM rate will appear after keying each line.

1   8489 19891 1919 1891 9981 19867 183218 189 19 698 98

2   99 88 589 998 998 888 991 999 498 98 99 88 94 32989 29

Key line 3 once and concentrate on control. Try to reach 25 WPM and make two or fewer errors (or follow the goals set by your instructor). Your WPM rate will appear after keying the line, and any errors will be highlighted.

3   23 1989 2239 39823 59891 123 698 92919 9812 375 688 9

**Exercise 16.12**    **1–9 Drill**

Complete the following drill to develop speed and concentration.

1   Key the numbers 1 through 9 three times. Space once between numbers and press Enter at the end of each number set. Keep your eyes on the screen.

2   Reverse the order and key the numbers 9 down through 1 three times. Space once between numbers and press Enter at the end of each number set. Again, keep your eyes on the screen.

**Exercise 16.13**    **0 (Zero) Drill**

Anchor the J finger on the home row as the ; (semicolon) finger keys 0. *Note: Be sure to use the* **zero** *key, not the capital* **O.**

Key the following line for speed. Try to reach 25 WPM (or the goal set by your instructor). Your WPM rate will appear after keying each line.

Key the line again for control. Try to reach 25 WPM and make two or fewer errors (or follow the goals set by your instructor). Your WPM rate will appear after keying the line, and any errors will be highlighted.

10 20 30 40 50 60 70 80 90 a10 a20 a30 240 250 10 115 619 057

**Exercise 16.14**    **1–100 Drill**

Key the numbers from 1 to 100. Space once between numbers.

**Exercise 16.15**    **Twos Drill**

Key the numbers 2 to 200 by twos (that is, key only even numbers). Space once between numbers.

**Exercise 16.16**    **Number Concentration Drill**

Key lines 1–5 once for control. Concentrate on reading the numbers in groups. Try to reach 25 WPM and make two or fewer errors (or follow the goals set by your instructor). After keying, your WPM rate and any errors will display.

1   11201 1316 14037 22304 3405 4506 35607 6708 78092 1415

2   6816z 62317 73218 2219 32206 8782 19222 90234 1929 3030

3   45317 7932 34332 13476 9535 87369 1370 1743 37744 7645

4   2674 65647 1674 84859 34750 25151 23270 45524 8910 573

5   91524 7853 85426 1927 52938 22304 11201 78092 7753 361

## Session
# 17
# Number Patterns, Columns of Numbers, and Number Style Guidelines

## Session Objectives

- **Explore and use number patterns**
- **Learn to use preset tabs to key columns of numbers**
- **Investigate style guidelines for expressing numbers**

## Getting Started

**Exercise 17.1**
If you are continuing immediately from Session 16, you may skip the Exercise 17.1 warm-up drill. However, if you exited the Online Lab at the end of Session 16, warm up by completing Exercise 17.1.

In addition to being a warm-up exercise, Exercise 17.1 provides an opportunity for further practice syllabizing numbers. Syllabizing helps you keep track of where you are in combinations of five or more numbers.

**Exercises 17.2–17.4**
Continue developing your number keyboarding skills by completing Exercises 17.2 through 17.4. Exercise 17.2 is a series of number drill lines, and Exercises 17.3 and 17.4 are text-based speed and accuracy drills. When keying drill lines for these exercises, follow the instruction prompts in the Online Lab.

## ➤➤ Reinforcing Your Skills

After working through the previous exercises, complete Exercises 17.5 through 17.13 in the Online Lab. Reference the drill lines from the textbook as you key and keep your eyes on the textbook pages, not on your fingers. Complete each exercise at least once, but repeat exercises if you want to improve your WPM rate or accuracy.

**Exercise 17.5**
### Numbers Drill

Key the following line for speed. Try to reach 25 WPM (or the goal set by your instructor). Your WPM rate will appear after keying the line.

Key the line again. This time, focus on control. Try to reach 25 WPM and make two or fewer errors (or follow the goals set by your instructor). Your WPM rate will appear after keying each line. Any errors will be highlighted. If either goal is not met, key the line again.

1  11 22 33 44 55 66 77 88 99 00

## Introducing the Comma and Decimal Point Keys

You have now been introduced to all 10 digits and are ready to review other areas of the keyboard. Two symbols used frequently with numbers are the comma (,) and the decimal point (.). The decimal point is also used as a period at the end of a sentence. These keys were presented in Session 3, but because they are used frequently with numbers, more practice is offered here.

**Videos 16.5–16.6**
The locations of the comma and decimal keys are shown in the following diagram. Watch Videos 16.5 through 16.6 and practice using these new keys.

**Exercises 16.17–16.20**
Complete Exercises 16.17 through 16.20 to learn to use these keys with numbers. When keying the drill lines, follow the instruction prompts in the Online Lab.

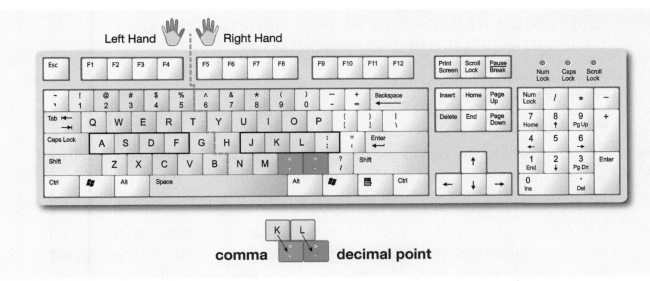

## Reinforcing Your Skills

Complete Exercises 16.21 through 16.24 in the Online Lab. Reference the drill lines from the textbook as you key and keep your eyes on the textbook pages, not on your fingers. Complete each exercise at least once, but repeat exercises if you want to improve your WPM rate or accuracy.

When numbers are separated by commas, decimals, spaces, letters, or other symbols, use those division points as natural breaks between groups of numbers. For example, 5,134 would be read as *five, comma, one thirty-four*.

**Exercise 16.21**  Comma Drill

Key lines 1 and 2 once for speed. Concentrate on grouping the numbers by division points. The comma is keyed with the middle finger of the right hand. Reach down from the K key. Try to reach 25 WPM (or the goal set by your instructor). Your WPM rate will appear after keying each line.

1  1,368 16,434 92,860 58,167 34,511 76,924 6,331 21,468

2  38,107 48,243 1,509 5,114 15,816 6,184,336 98,165,225

Key line 3 once and concentrate on control. Try to reach 25 WPM and make two or fewer errors (or follow the goals set by your instructor). Your WPM rate will appear after keying of the line, and any errors will be highlighted.

3  4,408,452 251,145 12,259 1,259 159,467 43,410 875,243

**Timing**
**16.2**
91 95 923 8466 9977 7898 69 45 239 945 966 9143 9 9123
5671 92345 3458 9612349 3467 12392 996 81389 5934278
59743219 11386519 2251396 973 99 9911319 9 5491 9375
19 2368 9 7629 947 61942 99111319 19 979 7426 5187 239

**Timing**
**16.3**
27 821 59361 40352 89734 92035 64019 9356 693 958 3177
501 6512 96 8742 56034 56832 85923 780 847 91 6409 7483
9467 3520 5945 2635 5705 8932 6485 1956 23670 81251800
165 208125635 69312 9871 6017340 2 716941 8320193 5163
8613 5113818 8542001 88490 6 2361 15432 11621618 11234
19051 3399 668 45441 4091 25937 68465 21893 492 591 783

Complete 1-minute timings on each of the paragraphs below. *Hint: Remember to press Tab at the start of each paragraph.*

1-Minute Timings

**Timing**
**16.4**
Zeb went to the zoo to see the 179 new animals. He went especially to see the 18 species of lizards. He wants to be a zoologist when he gets older. He knows many things about animals, and his parents are really amazed.

**Timing**
**16.5**
A cookout on the beach could include 6 kinds of cheese, carrots, 3 types of meat sandwiches, and 14 cans of cold juice. If the chill of the ocean is too much, hot chocolate and hot coffee can chase the cold chills. The decent lunch and a chat with friends can enrich affection.

**Timing**
**16.6**
An office clerk who lacks basic ethics could become the subject of scorn. Those who gossip about or verbally abuse new workers can cause problems. It is smart to follow the 13 rules that are printed on the bulletin board about getting along with fellow workers. Do the right thing and be sincere.

 **Ergonomic Tip**

The human body is made to move. When you stay in one position too long, you will end up stiff, sore, and stressed. After sitting at your workstation for 45–60 minutes, stand up and stretch your arms and legs.

## Ending the Session

The Online Lab automatically saved the work you completed for this session. You can continue with the next session or exit the Online Lab and continue later.

**Exercise 16.22**  Decimal Point Drill

Key lines 1 and 2 once for speed. Concentrate on reading numbers by division points. Try to reach 25 WPM (or the goal set by your instructor). Your WPM rate will appear after keying each line.

1  41,345.51 15,378.78 31,428.27 89,261,500.68 59.63 61.3

2  91,007.23 851,267.18 109.01 13.17 8.43 4.40 596.27 39.8

Key line 3 once and concentrate on control. Try to reach 25 WPM and make two or fewer errors (or follow the goals set by your instructor). Your WPM rate will appear after keying the line, and any errors will be highlighted.

3  990.85 67,349.34 23,265.08 186.84 4.23 .87 8,582 13.455

**Exercise 16.23**  Reinforcement Drill

Key lines 1 and 2 once for speed. Try to reach 25 WPM (or the goal set by your instructor). Your WPM rate will appear after keying each line.

1  77 77 7 7777 7777 777 777 77 77 7 7 7777 777 77 7

2  6 76 a555 677 777 77 a76 57 57 76 66 77 a55 75 75

Key line 3 once and concentrate on control. Try to reach 25 WPM and make two or fewer errors (or follow the goals set by your instructor). Your WPM rate will appear after keying the line, and any errors will be highlighted.

3  4651 1234 3467 461234 3457 56712 62345 5671 71234

Follow the previous *speed* instructions for lines 4–5, 7–8, and 10–11. Follow the previous *control* instructions for lines 6, 9, and 12.

4  88 88 88 88 88 888 888 88 88 8 8 8 88 88 88 8 8 8

5  8 11 88 11 688 11 88 11 88 11 88 11 588 11 88 411

6  88 2238 6818 71882 6817 2845 81828 8182 1482 8823

7  91 999 99 9 999 9 99 99 99 91 91 91 99 9 999 9 99

8  19 189 183218 19867 9981 1891 1919 19891 8489 989

9  92919 698 123 59891 39823 2239 1989 2923 32989 94

10  10 20 30 40 50 60 70 80 90 a10 a20 a30 240 250 10

11  6,151 6,719 1,438 4,497 5,313 7,893 38,751 45,134

12  .87 4.23 186.84 23,265.08 67,349.34 990.85 596.27

**Exercise** Sentence Drill
16.24
Key lines 1–10 once for speed. Try to reach 30 WPM (or the goal set by your instructor). Your WPM rate will appear after keying each line.

Key lines 1–10 again. This time, focus on control. Try to reach 30 WPM and make two or fewer errors (or follow the goals set by your instructor). Your WPM rate will appear after keying each line, and any errors will be highlighted.

1 Of the 15,220 rangers, 170 sprained their ankles last year.
2 Dirk did the drills first and drank the delicious tea later.
3 Take 12 or 13 fresh, green grapes as your dessert treat.

4 He risks great danger if he departs after the dinner.
5 The 14 interns gratefully lingered in the green garden.
6 The meat manager made a simple remark and smirked.

7 Did Mary send the 380 messages after amending them?
8 Pam had made some malts with milk, mint, and mango.
9 The firefighters attempted an immense task and missed.
10 Did Sammie eliminate the 16 mistakes in the message?

## Assessing Your Speed and Accuracy

Complete Timings 16.1 through 16.6 in the Online Lab to assess the skills you have learned in this session. Timings 16.1 through 16.3 will be timings on lines of numbers, and Timings 16.4 through 16.6 will be text-based paragraphs that include numbers. Refer to the following paragraphs as you key.

Each timing will start as soon as you begin keying. If you finish keying before the timing expires, press Enter and start keying the timing text again.

When time expires, the Online Lab will give you a WPM rate and will highlight any errors you made. The results will be stored in your Timings Performance Report.

*Hint: For the number timings, Timings 16.1 through 16.3, press Enter at the end of each line.*

1-Minute Timings

**Timing**
16.1
.81 85 823 8466 8877 7868 58 45 238 845 866 8143 8 8123
5671 82345 3458 8612348 3467 1238 886 81387 5834278
58743218 11386518 2251386 87 88 8811318 8 5481 8375
18 2368 8 7628 81 61842 8811318 18 8788 5792 6139 144